P9-DCP-843

Fairies

New and future titles in the series include:

Alien Abductions

Angels

Atlantis

The Bermuda Triangle

The Curse of King Tut

Dragons

Dreams

ESP

The Extinction of the Dinosaurs

Extraterrestrial Life

Fortune-Telling

Ghosts

Haunted Houses

The Kennedy Assassination

King Aurthur

The Loch Ness Monster

Pyramids

Stonehenge

UFOs

Unicorns

Vampires

Witches

The Mystery Library

Fairies

Nancy Hoffman

LUCENT
BOOKS®

THOMSON
————— ✳ ————— ™
GALE

San Diego • Detroit • New York • San Francisco • Cleveland • New Haven, Conn. • Waterville, Maine • London • Munich

On cover: A glowing fairy appears in John Atkinson Grimshaw's 1876 painting *Midsummer Night*.

© 2004 by Lucent Books. Lucent Books is an imprint of The Gale Group, Inc., a division of Thomson Learning, Inc.

Lucent Books® and Thomson Learning™ are trademarks used herein under license.

For more information, contact
Lucent Books
27500 Drake Rd.
Farmington Hills, MI 48331-3535
Or you can visit our Internet site at http://www.gale.com

ALL RIGHTS RESERVED.
No part of this work covered by the copyright hereon may be reproduced or used in any form or by any means—graphic, electronic, or mechanical, including photocopying, recording, taping, Web distribution, or information storage retrieval systems—without the written permission of the publisher.

LIBRARY OF CONGRESS CATALOGING-IN-PUBLICATION DATA

Hoffman, Nancy, 1955–
    Fairies / by Nancy Hoffman.
       v. cm. — (The mystery library)
Includes bibliographical references and index.
Contents: What are fairies?—The origins of fairy folk—The evolution of the fairy faith—Human encounters with fairies—The search for fairies.
    ISBN 1-56006-973-2 (alk. paper)
1. Fairies—Juvenile literature. [1. Fairies.] I. Title. II. Mystery library (Lucent Books).
    BF1552.H64 2004
    133.1'4—dc22

                       2003006836

Printed in the United States of America

Contents

Foreword

In Shakespeare's immortal play, *Hamlet*, the young Danish aristocrat Horatio has clearly been astonished and disconcerted by his encounter with a ghost-like apparition on the castle battlements. "There are more things in heaven and earth," his friend Hamlet assures him, "than are dreamt of in your philosophy."

Many people today would readily agree with Hamlet that the world and the vast universe surrounding it are teeming with wonders and oddities that remain largely outside the realm of present human knowledge or understanding. How did the universe begin? What caused the dinosaurs to become extinct? Was the lost continent of Atlantis a real place or merely legendary? Does a monstrous creature lurk beneath the surface of Scotland's Loch Ness? These are only a few of the intriguing questions that remain unanswered, despite the many great strides made by science in recent centuries.

Lucent Books' Mystery Library series is dedicated to exploring these and other perplexing, sometimes bizarre, and often disturbing or frightening wonders. Each volume in the series presents the best-known tales, incidents, and evidence surrounding the topic in question. Also included are the opinions and theories of scientists and other experts who have attempted to unravel and solve the ongoing mystery. And supplementing this information is a fulsome list of sources for further reading, providing the reader with the means to pursue the topic further.

The Mystery Library will satisfy every young reader's fascination for the unexplained. As one of history's greatest scientists, physicist Albert Einstein, put it:

> The most beautiful thing we can experience is the mysterious. It is the source of all true art and science. He to whom this emotion is a stranger, who can no longer wonder and stand rapt in awe, is as good as dead: his eyes are closed.

The Little People of the Countryside

Fairies and fairylike beings are found in cultures around the world, particularly in the British Isles where fairy faith has long been associated with ancient Celtic beliefs. Fairies have been part of Britain's supernatural heritage for at least fifteen hundred years. At times, fairies were considered remnants of ancient pagan faiths and a source of evil. At other times, these mystical beings were thought of as good and gentle, secretly helping and inspiring deserving individuals. Most believers think fairies possess both good and bad traits, dealing with the human world at the fairies' whims.

Connected to the human world through the mysteries of nature and creativity, fairies are believed to thrive in rural countrysides. But as nature becomes overrun by mankind, it seems little room is left for the fairies. In the mid–nineteenth century, Scottish geologist and writer Hugh Miller reported that all the fairies had left Scotland. In his book *Old Red Sandstone*, Miller writes that it happened on a Sunday morning around noon. A shepherd boy and his sister watched as a troop of tattered little people

This drawing depicts a male fairy flitting about the upper branches of a tree. Fairies are believed to reside in the natural world, far from civilization.

marched wearily out of a ravine and through a wooded hollow, disappearing over a hill. They wore old, plaid cloaks and red caps. Their scraggly hair stuck out wildly, making them look even more disheveled. Some rode tiny, gray-speckled horses. The shepherd boy yelled to one little man in the sad brigade, "What are ye, little mannie? and where are ye going?" The small man answered, "Not of the race of Adam." Then he turned in his saddle and said, "The People of Peace [the fairies] shall never more be seen in Scotland."[1] Miller's account of the fairies' exodus continues to be contradicted by the scores of people who claim to have encountered fairies in Scotland and throughout the world. Perhaps as a reaction to the loss of rural countryside, the belief in and respect for fairies—the mystical guardians of the natural world—grows.

What Are Fairies?

People meet fairies and fairylike beings in subtle yet fantastic ways. Fairies constantly alter their appearance, making them difficult to identify. One moment happy and helpful, the next angry and vengeful, fairies' emotions are always changing, making them even more difficult to understand. What people believe about them comes from legends, stories passed down through many generations, and personal accounts of mystical and mysterious experiences. These are the fairies, and they are not easy to define.

Most people imagine fairies look like Walt Disney's animated version of Tinkerbell, a tiny humanoid with wings, but fairies are believed to be as diverse in appearance as they are in nature. Mermaids, the fairies of the oceans, have fish tails, webbed hands, and long red or green hair identical to strands of seaweed. The evil fairies of Scotland, sometimes referred to as the *slaugh*, look like hordes of hideous skeletons ravaging the countryside on bitterly cold winter nights. Many claim to have seen Native American little people resembling miniature humans hugging cliffs or among the rocks of river rapids in the United States. But however they appear, all fairies share the following four traits: the ability to do magic, the ability to materialize from their natural state of invisibility, a strong connection to nature, and possession of human social characteristics.

Fairy Size

Fairies are often thought of as tiny beings. With flowing pastel clothing, impish expressions, and translucent wings, flower fairies could easily be confused with butterflies in a garden. Rings of inch-high toadstools are believed to host fairy dances. Even the different names for fairies—elves, little people, nixies—sound small. Some folklorists believe fairies are thought of as little in size because they are often associated with Britain's prehistoric earth dwellings like cramped caves.

Not all who believe in fairies agree on the size of these mysterious beings. Fairy size, as with other elements of fairy appearance, is the choice of the fairies. How tall a fairy stands often has to do with the amount of pride and power it possesses or wants to portray to mortals. Fairies who marry humans are always thought of as being human-size, while some are thought to be much bigger than people. George William Russell, a well-known mystic in the early 1900s, believed the Sidhe, Ireland's royal fairies, were at least as tall as humans and quite spectacular in appear-

An illustration depicts fairies as tiny beings. However, many believers contend that fairies are as tall as, or even taller than, humans.

ance. In an interview with folklorist W.Y. Evans Wentz, Russell describes what he and others believed about the Sidhe's size and appearance:

> The shining beings seem to be about our own stature or just a little taller. Peasant and other Irish seers do not usually speak of the Sidhe as being little but as being tall: an old schoolmaster in the West of Ireland described them to me from his own visions as tall beautiful people, and he used some Gaelic [ancient Irish] words, which I took as meaning they were shining with every colour.[2]

Others interviewed by Evans Wentz agreed with Russell. An Irish sailor named Michael Reddy told Evans Wentz he saw the Sidhe at Lower Rosses Point in Ireland: "I first saw them like an officer pointing at me what seemed a sword; and when I got on the Greenlands I saw a great company of gentry, like soldiers, in red, laughing and shouting. Their leader was a big man and they were ordinary human size."[3]

Size, shape, and all other qualities of appearance are questionable when dealing with the fairies. But like people, most fairies live in groups similar to human societies.

Fairy Royalty

Like human beings, fairies also rank themselves by power, privilege, and status. There are leaders and followers and many inbetween in the fairy world just as there are in the human world.

The trooping fairies are the fairy royalty of the British Isles. They have royal courts with kings, queens, and knights and are believed to patrol the countryside like a small medieval army.

The Seelie and UnSeelie Courts of Scotland are good examples of the best and worst of fairy monarchies. Fairies from the Seelie Court live peacefully beside humans. Their

A fairy king and queen lead a procession among their subjects. Fairy society is extremely class conscious and is governed as a monarchy.

noble members love to hunt, feast, and dance. Traditionally, Seelie Court revelry is best observed on clear summer nights. The UnSeelie Court, however, appears in the dead of winter to wreak havoc upon the landscape. They are the evil fairies of Scottish folklore. Appearing like a huge dark cloud blowing past a cold winter's sky, this evil fairy court has been thought to recruit minor criminals and vagrants to its ranks. Many believe members of the UnSeelie Court cause sickness and death in domestic animals and humans.

Just as several monarchies have disappeared in the human world, many believe the trooping fairies have left Great Britain. Many accounts of dwindling royal fairy courts were given long before geologist Hugh Miller wrote about the fairies' departure from Scotland in the early 1800s. In *The Canterbury Tales*, fourteenth-century English poet Geoffrey Chaucer wrote that the fairies had long left the British Isles. Other stories claim ringing church bells drove the fairy courts away. Folklorist Katherine Briggs, however, believes rumors of fairies leaving are balanced by accounts of fairy sightings. In her book *The Vanishing*

People Briggs wrote: "One is told anecdotes of their being seen in such sophisticated places as Kensington Gardens or rural Surrey. The fairies, older than the oldest gods of whom we have mythological records, still show here and there a flicker of their former life."[4] These most aristocratic fairies travel in nighttime royal processions called fairy rades. The rades, short for parades, are royal excursions in which members of fairy monarchies show off all their splendor.

House or Servant Fairies

While most fairies travel in groups, occasionally revealing their splendor to the world, a few live simply by themselves in and around human dwellings. They are known as the house fairies or house elves. One belief about house fairies is that they descended from the house gods and spirits of ancient religions. People still make offerings to these spirits hoping they will bless their homes and crops. Other views suggest house fairies act as servants to housemasters. Their powers are used to perform domestic and agricultural tasks. These fairies cook, make clothing, clean barns, grind grain, and harvest crops at speeds and in quantities human beings could only imagine. In *L'Allegro*, English poet John Milton wrote about a feat of a house fairy whose flail made short work of harvested corn:

> When in one night, ere glimpse of morn
> His shadowy Flale hath thresh'd the Corn
> That ten day-labourers could not end.[5]

The best-known house elf is the English brownie, who some believe was exiled from fairy royalty before becoming a house spirit. Katherine Briggs writes how the brownies' love of new clothes is evidence that this house elf is actually an exile from the fairy court. According to Briggs, legends imply that the brownie could return to royal fairy revelry if he acquired fine new clothes. Therefore, tradition dictates

A house elf eats beside the stove during the family's dinner. Many variations of the house fairy exist in folklore around the world.

a sure way to rid a home of a brownie is to present the elf with any article of clothing. J.K. Rowling's version of the English brownie, Dobby the house elf, was freed from servitude to the evil Malfoy family when accidently given one of his master's socks in Rowling's novel *Harry Potter and the Chamber of Secrets.*

Not all household fairies work as hard as the English brownie. The *tomtra*, from the folklore of Finland, torments household residents into becoming tidy. While the *tomtra* does some work, he also expects family members to learn from him to keep their homes immaculate. The *tomtra* also demands food and shelter year-round and gifts at Christmastime. If the human residents of a *tomtra*-inhabited house do not straighten up, the *tomtra* will leave, taking away any luck the family might have had.

According to legend, the duendes of Spain and Latin America look like middle-aged women. They also clean houses, but they do not bring luck to the homes they inhabit; the cleaning the duendes do is only for their own comfort. Like ghostly spirits, the duendes throw pots and pans and move furniture in an effort to scare family members into leaving the home. It is very difficult to rid a home of a duende.

The small kitchen fairy of China is always industrious—obsessively scrubbing, sweeping, and dusting. The cleanest homes in China are believed to have kitchen fairies hard at work. The only problem with kitchen fairies is the payment they require from the head of a household for a year's labor: one human to eat. However, since kitchen fairies are believed to be rather stupid, they can easily be fooled. By breaking pottery and claiming the damage to be the fairy's fault, heads of households can postpone payment for several years and keep these fairies trapped in servitude. To avoid kitchen fairies, people are encouraged to leave small amounts of water in all their pots to keep these tiny household sprites from living in the pots.

Even fairies who live in and around human homes are not likely to be seen by the human residents. While humans can sometimes see fairies in disguise, few see fairies in their true form, for it appears that fairies cannot be seen unless they want to be seen.

To See a Fairy

It is not in a fairy's nature to be seen by humans. When fairies do appear, it is often as quick as a glance. They do this to confuse mortals and to amuse themselves. According to folklorist Katherine Briggs, tradition dictates those lucky enough to see fairies can do so only "between one eye blink and the next."[6] In fact, English children were scolded against staring in public with the admonition that staring was an attempt to "watch the fairies." As Brian Froud, author of several books on fairies, wrote:

> No one can introduce you to faeries, . . . they will either accept you as a part of their world, or they won't. It's up to them. . . . Sometimes no amount of mooning around in misty forest glades or communing with nature at the bottom of the garden (erroneously said to be a favourite haunt of faeries) will bring about anything other than a general sense of damp.[7]

Perhaps the only way to see fairies is to be sensitive and positive about their existence and wait for them to come to you. The Irish poet William Butler Yeats (1865–1939) claimed to have seen fairies and to have been influenced by them many times. Yeats believed how and when people see fairies is determined as much by human feelings toward fairies as by the fairies' impulses. To Yeats, fairies have "no inherent form, but change according to their whim or the mind that sees them. You can not lift your hand without influencing and being influenced by hordes of faeries."[8]

In a Different Dimension

There are many explanations for fairies' changeable appearances, invisibility, and love of trickery. Robert Kirk, an Episcopalian minister in the seventeenth century, claimed to have discovered a Celtic kingdom of Scottish fairies. Kirk's experience with the fairies convinced him that the mystical beings had humanlike intelligence, supernormal powers, and were invisible to all but those with the "second sight," or the ability to see purely spiritual beings. Kirk

Fairy Funeral

Most people believe fairies are immortal and therefore do not die. English poet and artist William Blake, however, once spoke of a particularly unusual fairy sighting. He claimed to have watched a fairy funeral. Carole G. Silver gives an account of Blake's vision in her book *Strange and Secret Peoples: Fairies and Victorian Consciousness.* According to Silver, Blake was discussing fairies with a woman sitting next to him at a dinner party. He asked her if she ever saw any fairies. When she said she did not think so, he proceeded to tell her about one of his alleged encounters with the mystical sprites.

I was walking alone in my garden; there was great stillness among the branches and

flowers, and more than common sweetness in the air; I heard a low and pleasant sound, and I knew not whence it came. At last, I saw the broad leaf of a flower move, and underneath I saw a procession of creatures, of the size and colour of green and grey grasshoppers, bearing a body laid out on a rose leaf, which they buried with songs and then disappeared.

Blake's art, painted in the early 1800s, laid the foundation for later works that depicted the fairies. Fairies and other supernatural beings were the subjects of many of Blake's works. In them, fairies looked human and seemed to exhibit human attitudes.

wrote that fairies are "of a middle nature betwixt man and angel. . . . [They have] light changeable bodies, somewhat of the nature of a condensed cloud and best seen at twilight."[9]

Kirk's ideas concerning the fairies became popular when Theosophists adopted them. Theosophists, followers of a religious philosphy widely practiced in the mid-1800s to the early 1900s, believe there are different dimensions or worlds where mystical and spiritual beings like fairies dwell. Theosophists believe that because fairies inhabit a higher, more refined, and sensitive dimension of thought, most people are unaware of their existence. According to George William Russell, people find fairies with their minds, not their eyes: "In seeing these beings of which I speak, the physical eyes may be open or closed; mystical beings in their own world and nature are never seen with the physical eyes."[10] To Theosophists, fairies are more than just nature spirits. They are energy developed from higher thoughts and emotions.

Fairy Magic

The word *fairy* derives from the French word *fey*, which means enchantment. Fairies enchant humans by manipulating their senses and the natural world around them.

Fairy magic spells sometimes help people, as in the tale of Bill Doody. As told for generations in Ireland, poor Bill Doody sat by the shores of Lake Killarney, wondering how he was going to pay his rent. Out of nowhere, a tall gentleman plopped a bag of gold into Bill Doody's hat. The man, who was really Prince O'Donoghue, the leader of the lake fairies, vanished before Bill Doody could thank him. Bill Doody then went to his landlord, paid his rent with the gold and received a receipt. After Bill Doody left, the landlord went to deposit the gold and found nothing but gingerbread cakes shaped like coins in its place. The landlord could not collect more from Bill Doody since Bill Doody

A photo shows a fairy ring of toadstools, a magical place where, some say, fairies sing and dance. Humans who step into such a ring risk falling under a fairy spell.

had a receipt. From that day forward, Bill Doody's luck changed. He became happy, healthy, and wealthy.

Not all encounters with fairies, however, are marked by such generosity and kindliness. Fairy spells can also harm humans, as in one Scottish legend about a man who had the misfortune to fall asleep in a fairy ring, which is a circle of plants or toadstools where fairies come out and dance. When the man awoke, he was being rapidly pulled through the air. Then he was dropped in the middle of Glasgow many miles from his home near Selkirk. His hat and coat had been taken and he had nothing to protect him against the cold. He was lucky to come across someone who knew him and could take him back to Selkirk.

Sometimes fairies are known to play tricks that neither help nor seriously harm anyone. In 1879, folklorist Wil-

Chapter 1: What Are Fairies?

liam Henderson wrote about a house fairy named Kow who delighted in disturbing a northern England farm-house. Through magic trickery, Kow overturned pots, unravelled knitting, and left all the cream out for the cats. Such playful pestering is common in many fairy stories.

Fairy Time

Fairies perform other magic beyond giving away enchanted gold, providing unexpected travels, and playing tricks. They can also manipulate time and place. Stories abound of fairies bewitching people and taking them into other worlds. Time passes differently in these magical places—what seems like a few days turns out to be one hundred years in human time, or what seems like a month actually is only a moment.

The tale of a shepherd from Pembrokeshire, England, is a good example of time passing slowly in fairyland. A young lad joined a group of fairies dancing in a fairy ring. When the dancing ended, the fairies took him to a beautiful garden with a well in its center where silver and gold fish swam. He was told he could stay there as long as he wanted providing he never drank water from the well. Eventually, after months seemed to have passed, temptation got the better of him and he cupped his hands while reaching for the water. When he touched it, he heard a loud shrill noise and immediately was transported back to a hillside surrounded by his father's sheep. He had been away no more than a hour of human time.

Fairy time passed quickly in the story of two famous fiddlers who were staying at an Iverness inn during Christmas. A small, old, but elegantly dressed man asked the two men if they could play at a nearby gathering. The musicians agreed and the old gentleman led them to a strange, rough tower. As they walked inside, the rustic exterior fell away to reveal a splendid palace. The people gathered there were all elegantly dressed and beautiful. The musicians played all night, never tiring. The next morning, walking away from the tower, they noticed it was no more than a low hill. They did not recognize anyone and no one recognized them as they walked back to town. Everything around them looked different from what they recalled a day ago. Eventually they realized one hundred years had passed since they entered the fairy hill. Happy to have survived this fairy enchantment, they wandered into a church. At the first reading of scripture, the two fiddlers crumbled into dust.

The kind of fairy magic that manipulates objects and time confuses and confounds mortals. Some fairy magic totally bewitches people, changing their lives forever. It is this magic that distorts human perception.

Fairy Glamour

Glamour is often a trait that people today associate with beautiful movie stars. However, glamour has a different meaning in connection with fairies. Commonly linked with temptation, glamour is the power fairies have to "enchant" people into seeing something that is not real. As Reginald Scot's poem "The Lay of the Last Minstrel" states, glamour

> Could Make a ladye seem a knight,
> A nutshell seem a gilded barge
> A sheeling seem a palace large
> And youth seem age and age seem youth
> All was delusion, nought was truth.[11]

Accounts of beautiful fairies enchanting mortal men can be found in many different cultures. The men, captivated by these luminous beings, quickly fall in love with them and fall under their spells. In many stories, men are enticed to their doom by such "glamourous" fairies.

Fairy glamour is also used to trick humans into believing things are different than they actually are. Brian Froud, author of several books on fairies, writes about his frustration with never being sure about anything concerning the fairies, even their food: "Who is to divine [determine] with authority whether that silver goblet of heavenly mead is not an acorn filled with brackish water; that those royal banquet tables groaning under the weight of rare delicacies are not solely poor platters of faded autumn leaves, those luscious plums toadstools."[12]

The belief in fairies being able to misrepresent reality through glamour sometimes results in dire consequences for mortals. Glamour has even been used as an excuse for violence against human beings. In 1894 in Clonmel, Ireland, a man named Cleary tortured and killed a woman most people thought to be his wife, Brigit. In his defense,

Fairies often enchant mortal men with their beauty. Stories of men falling under the spell of fairies are found in many different cultures.

Cleary argued that his "real" wife had been taken by the fairies and the woman left in his home was actually a block of wood enchanted by glamour to act and speak like his wife. Cleary's legal strategy, however, did not work and he was convicted of murder.

Fairy glamour is only one way to trick humans. Fairies also alter their size and form to avoid being identified. That power is called shape shifting.

Shape Shifting

Shape shifting is the fairies' ability to drastically and instantly change their form. They can suddenly become very tall, almost giant size, then shrink to the size of an insect; and then totally disappear.

Fairies can change their color and take on any disguise they like. They can become human, animal, or even a plant or tree. As playwright William Shakespeare wrote in *The Merry Wives of Windsor,*

> Fairies, black, grey, green and white,
> You moonshine revellers and shades of night.[13]

Shape shifting is extremely important to fairy life because it is one way fairies maintain or regain their invisibility while playing tricks on humans. There are countless tales of fairies escaping human sight by changing into animals. The *lutins*, gnomelike fairies from Brittany, France, reportedly turn into black horses or goats to confuse and trick nighttime travelers. Fairy women have been known to turn into deer to lure hunters to fairy palaces. Irish warrior fairies often take on the appearance of birds during battle to confuse the enemy and better observe the action.

Part of the Four Elements

Besides watching over and living within nature, fairies are also thought to reflect the energy behind nature's forces and its four elements: earth, water, fire, and air.

Earth fairies reflect the power, resources, and cycles of nature and rule over the ancient hills and rocky terrain of the earth. Earth fairies such as the Native American little people are believed to bring good crops and game animals to feed members of the Cherokee, Iroquois, and Seneca nations. Other earth fairies like the gnomes of German mythology are believed to be hard at work underground. The gnomes are among the miners of the fairy world— hammering away under hills and in caves harvesting the earth's minerals and gems. Earth fairies can also be playful like Scandinavia's wood wives and eastern Europe's *veela*, who dance and frolic through forests, dressing the trees for each new season.

Water fairies symbolize intuition and transformation. Their ranks include mermaids, *selkies*, *merrows*, and other water-dwelling spirits. Tales of water fairies teach respect for the water and its hazards. Seeing a water fairy is often a warning to sailors and fishermen of rough waters ahead. Water fairies are usually beautiful and sometimes that beauty hides treachery. For example, the nixies often lure men to their deaths in the hidden undercurrents and whirlpools of rivers and lakes in Scandinavia, Germany, and Switzerland. Some water fairies, however, help humans. There are many tales of mermaids saving people from drowning. Mermaids are believed to come ashore and hide their fish scales and fish tails within the sand and rocks. While walking on land, their webbed fingers disappear. There are stories of mortal men even marrying mermaids. Similarly, the *selkies* and *merrows* of the British Isles transform from seals in the sea to humanlike beings on land. *Selkies* and *merrows* also have been known to marry humans. Some are also thought to become the changeling children of humans.

Fire fairies are symbols of the destruction and rejuvenation associated with the cycle of nature. Followers of ancient British religions called upon the fire fairies to light huge

Mermaids are beautiful water fairies that save humans from drowning. Different types of fairies are associated with each of nature's four basic elements.

bonfires for celebrations honoring the seasons. According to these pagan faiths, fairies spring from the fire's flames on wings of pure energy. Fire fairies are also thought to oversee the hearth (or fireplace) in homes—providing heat to cook food and to keep families warm in the winter.

Air fairies represent freedom and transcendence from earthly thoughts and deeds. They are also the messengers of the fairy world. Air fairies travel through the skies on wings warning of storms and impending death. Some, like the Irish banshees, let out loud wails proclaiming the death of a family member. Others, like Spain's El Nubero, cause storms. According to legend, El Nubero lives on the highest peak in North Africa where he and his family send out violent winds and rain across the Mediterranean Sea to the Spanish coast.

Human Qualities

Those who believe in fairies have also presumed that these mystical beings have human qualities. And those who claim to have encountered fairies have witnessed evidence of these human qualities. Just like people, fairies can be both good and bad depending upon their moods.

Fairies are thought to be curious, especially about humans and the human world. Ann Moura, author of *Green Witchcraft: Folk Magic, Fairy Lore and Herb Craft*, writes: "You can tell that you have attracted the fairies to

Winged fairies and menacing goblins hover over a sleeping girl. Fairies are curious creatures who like to explore the human world.

your home when things disappear for awhile then turn up unexpectedly. They are very curious and will borrow things to use or to examine but will return them in due time."[14]

Fairies also tend to be quite judgmental, dispensing their own brand of justice upon those whose behavior does not meet their moral standards. Fairies hate laziness and sloppiness. Many people believe those who keep dirty, cluttered homes are at risk of fairy punishment. Disapproving fairies might inflict muscle cramps, aching bones, or even lameness on unsuspecting humans. Fairies approve of and reward the generous and grateful. Many people leave food and drink out at night for the fairies. In return, they believe they are blessed with good luck, good health, and prosperity.

Fairy personalities are changeable and vary greatly from one group to the next. Many fairies are vain and self-serving like the Irish Sidhe who love beauty, insist upon luxury, and abhor frugality. Other fairies, like the house elves of the British Isles, are hardworking and thrifty, rarely throwing anything away.

Ever elusive, magical, and mysterious, fairies often defy explanation. But perhaps it is the fairies' changeable nature that helps them adapt to an ever-changing world, while faith in their existence and power continues to survive and evolve from its very early origins.

Chapter 2

The Origins of Fairy Folk

Beliefs, myths, and superstitions concerning where fairies come from are as diverse as the fairies themselves. According to the creator of Peter Pan, J.M. Barrie: "When the first baby laughed for the first time, his laugh broke into a million pieces and they all went skipping about. That was the beginning of fairies."[15] Belief in fairies and fairylike spirits, however, precedes the creation of Barrie's Tinkerbell by thousands of years. How those beliefs developed is not known, but many theories exist. In his book *Celtic Lore*, John Rhys writes, "I should hesitate to do anything so rash as to pronounce the fairies to be all of one and the same origin; they may well be of several."[16] Historians and archaeologists claim that many cultures shared beliefs in fairylike beings even before any known religions existed.

Ancestor Worship

The earliest beliefs in fairies are thought to concern ancestor worship. As the name implies, ancestor worship is honoring relatives who have died. In many ancient cultures, the dead became spirits with special powers that could be used to change the lives of the living. In these societies, ancestors with heroic qualities obtain godlike status when they die. Japan's earliest religion, Shinto, is a good example of ancestor

This painting depicts the death of Alexander the Great (reclining, top right). According to legend, the military leader now lives with the Nereids, the sea fairies of Greek mythology.

worship. According to Shinto doctrines, the Japanese people descended from a sun god and goddess. When some Shinto heroes die, they are believed to join the gods and goddesses and watch over the living.

Several European myths claim that when many well-known heroes die they go to live with the fairies. According to legend, Alexander the Great, the Greek military leader who conquered the Persian empire in 336 B.C., lives with Nereids, the sea fairies of ancient Greek mythology. Similarly, the Scandinavian king, Olaf, was thought to have become the Elf of Geirstad after he died. Folklorists in the early 1900s found many people in the British Isles who also thought dead heroes became fairies. In *The Fairy Faith in Celtic Countries*, W.Y. Evans Wentz reported on one such interview with Irishman John Graham. "People killed and murdered in wars, stay on earth till their time is

up and they are among the good people [the fairies],"
Graham told an early–twentieth-century researcher.
"The souls on this earth are as thick as the grass, and you
can't see them."[17] One local Irish legend alleges that the
sixteenth-century warrior Hugh O'Neil was joined in
victorious battle by the spirits of ancestors who lived at
the Rath of Ringlestown.

In Great Britain, many believe that common people—
not merely heroes—join the ranks of the fairies when they
die. The Irish tale of the tacksman of Auchriachan de-
monstrates this belief. The tacksman, or herding boy, went
looking for stray goats when a mist fell over the land.
When it cleared, he saw a strange-looking house that
seemed to almost be part of the hill. He was at once convinced it was a fairy house in a fairy hill. He knocked on
the door and a woman he recognized answered it; he had
attended her funeral a couple of months earlier.

Fairy pixies, or *piskies*, are also thought to be spirits of
the dead. Speaking of the mystical beings who inhabit the
Isle of Man, folklorist Sophia Morrison writes: "A great
deal was said about ghosts in this place. Whether or not
piskies are the same as ghosts, I cannot tell, but I fancy the
old folk thought they were."[18]

In some cultures, fairylike spirits of the dead help
humans in essential ways. According to legend, the Maori
people of New Zealand learned how to fish from ghostly
fairies called *patupairehe*. One day a man came upon the
remains of fish that had been cleaned. The man thought
that people would not abandon such a catch but that spirits
might. The man waited until evening when the *patupairehe*
came to claim the catch and fish some more. Without
being noticed, the man joined the fairies in their work. He
worked with them all night learning how to make fishing
nets and how to properly throw the nets and string fish.
When he had trouble collecting fish because his string was
too short, the fairies taught him how to do it correctly.

Before dawn, the fairies collected their fish and the man collected what he had caught. The man took what he learned back to the Maori people, and today the Maori are known as great fishermen.

Nature-Based Religions

Different cultures and different religions developed separate myths about major and minor deities and spirits of nature. Ancient peoples often believed the world was controlled by invisible magical powers. Often these were attributed to supernatural beings such as gods and goddesses. Many fairies, then, descended from these gods and goddesses of ancient religions. The earliest belief systems usually included myths about the creation of the world, natural phenomena, and life after death. Gods, goddesses, and fairies were main characters in these myths.

A myth from the southwestern United States explains how two little men saved the Hopi Indians from the Wind God. The Hopi were unhappy because constant wind blew away the seeds they were trying to plant. So they called upon the little people for help. The two little men who came to their aid agreed to go to the Wind God and give him offerings from the Hopi. Along the way, the little fellows got some sweet cornmeal mush from a being known as Spider Woman. When they reached Sunset Crater, where the Wind God lived, they located a passage into the earth. The men threw in the offerings and then threw in the rest of the cornmeal. These tokens sealed the door to the Wind God's lair. The wind no longer blew and it grew hot as a result. The Hopi once again called upon the little fellows to help them overcome the heat. The little men journeyed back to Sunset Crater. Once there they made a hole in the seal and out came a cool breeze which blew over all the Hopi. Ever since that time, the Hopi have called upon the little fellows during the windy month of March to perform the same rituals and contend with the Wind God.

While often thought of as part of another world, fairies are still guardians over this one. They symbolize mankind's relationship with nature. "Faeries are the inner nature of the land and a reflection of the inner nature of our souls,"[19] writes fairy scholar Brian Froud. Fairies are thought to reside in natural stone forts, within the earth's caves and hills, around lonely rings of plants or toadstools, or in the ancient trees of the British Isles. Often in Britain, an old oak, elm, or elder tree is considered good luck because it shelters good fairies. According to some European folklore, fairies take on the appearance of their natural habitat. Folklorist Katherine Briggs describes the wood elves of Scandinavia as having hollowed backs "like the trunk of a hollow tree."[20] As caretakers of their habitats, fairies are believed to protect plants and animals and guard fresh bodies of water. Scotland's Blue Hag of Winter is thought to beat her staff to bring snow to replenish mountain streams. Many people believe she also protects the wild mountain animals including deer, mountain goats, and wolves. The

Rumpelstiltskin

In the folklore of Germany, Rumpelstiltskin is an ugly elf who helps a miller's daughter spin straw into gold. By accomplishing this task, the girl can marry a king and become his queen. In payment for his help, Rumpelstiltskin asks for the girl's firstborn child. Years later the girl, who is now queen, gives birth to a son, and Rumpelstiltskin appears to claim the infant. The queen pleads with the elf to forego the payment. Eventually he agrees that if she can guess his real name within three days, she can keep her child. The queen tries unsuccessfully for two days, growing more disheartened as her time runs out. On the morning of the third day, the queen's servant overhears the elf singing his name. The servant quickly tells the distraught queen. When Rumpelstiltskin comes to collect the queen's child, he screams in horror when the now-confident queen utters the elf's name. Rumplestiltskin flees the kingdom and is never seen again. Characters similar to Rumpelstiltskin can be found in folklore all across Europe, and the bargaining aspect of the elf's nature is also common to many fairy stories.

The ancient Greeks believed that nymphs, such as these wood nymphs, protected the trees and rivers in which they lived. Nymphs severely punished those who did not respect nature.

Brown Man of the Muirs is the guardian spirit of wild game and wildlife on the Scottish Moors.

In appreciation for the fairies' caretaking, people began to pay tribute to these nature spirits. Some people would leave gifts of food or drink out for the fairies. Others learned to ask the fairies' permission before they collected natural resources. In many different cultures, people asked for the fairies' help by reciting special verses of poems. Avoiding these rituals was often considered dangerous.

Superstition dictates those who do not properly acknowledge the nymphs run the risk of their wrath. Nymphs are thought of as the fairies of ancient Greece. The word *nymph* means beautiful and fertile woman. The nymphs are believed to protect the trees, springs, and rivers that they supposedly inhabit in Greece's rocky countryside. Before taking a drink of water from a spring, most Greek shepherds would ask permission from the nymph living there, fearing if they did not, they could be bitten by a water snake or worse. The same logic applies to those who think about cutting down a tree in

Greece. If they believe as the ancients did, they could be harming a wood nymph who would seek revenge.

Honoring nature spirits and relying on their supernatural powers for help also became a basis for the ancient Celtic religion, which once thrived throughout Europe. Remnants of this faith can still be found in the British Isles today.

The Magic of the Ancient Celtic Faith

The earliest societies known to believe in fairies practiced ancient pagan religions. Pagans worship many different gods and goddesses. Besides the ancient Greeks and Romans, these early societies included the Celts, from which the native people of the British Isles descended. The people of the British Isles have long claimed fairies as part of their mythology. The ancient Celts worshiped fairies as sacred gods and goddesses and as powerful inhabitants and protectors of nature. Fairy encyclopedist Pierre Dubois claims the fairies were the souls of sage advisers, or Druids, of ancient Celtic societies. "Before returning to this world

Ancient Celts sacrifice cattle in a pagan ritual. The Celts were among the earliest people to worship fairies as sacred deities.

to inhabit other bodies, these chosen souls traveled to another kingdom where they lived for thousands of years under the transparent guise of phantoms. Female druids on earth, they were faeries in heaven,"[21] Dubois writes.

Little is known about the ancient Celtic religion except that poetry, magic, and nature were very important elements of its rituals. This ancient fairy faith placed a strong emphasis on the power and divinity of nature. The Celts believed their priests and priestesses understood the secrets of nature because they possessed the skills to communicate with the fairies. This communication took the form of oral poetry. Sometimes priests, called bards, told epic poems about Celtic heroes, gods and goddesses, and fairy folk. In part, these poetic legends often explained natural phenomena by attributing them to the actions of these mystical beings or to the powers of the fairies themselves.

All Celtic priests and priestesses were well schooled in the art of magic. To the Celts, magic was the ability to work with the fairy spirits to better control the world around them. There were two schools of magic—white and black. Black magic was rarely used and was only for selfish and evil ends. White magic was used in ancient religious ceremonies for the good of the people and the community. Poetry was one tool Celtic priests used to perform white magic. In ancient rituals and celebrations, the priests would recite a verse that often sounded like a magic incantation. These spells would call upon the fairies to bring about the needed magic—whether to heal the sick or provide an abundant harvest. Thus, fairies were considered the main source of magic for the priests and priestesses of ancient pagan religions. And as Dubois contends, many ancients believed these priests and priestesses became fairies when they died.

Fairy Origin and Greek Mythology

The ancient Greek gods and goddesses had much in common with Celtic fairies. The many Greek minor gods and goddesses paralleled Celtic fairies in their powers and their temperaments. The Greek god of nature, Pan, is a good example of a fairylike deity. Covered in shaggy hair with pointy ears, small horns on his head, and goat legs, Pan was so ugly that his mother, a nymph, abandoned him right after he was born. But his father, the god Hermes, had an immediate fondness for his strange-looking son, and he carried him up to Mount Olympus, where Pan entertained the most powerful gods and goddesses by playing music. Eventually he was sent back to Earth where he watched over hunters and shepherds and their sheep.

On moonlit nights, Pan could be found playing a shepherd's flute, followed by other mythological beings like the satyrs and the nymphs. Such depictions of Pan's nighttime parties resemble stories of fairy revelry from other parts of the world.

A sculpture of Pan, the Greek god of nature, shows his horns and goat legs. Many Greek deities exhibit fairylike qualities.

Pan's appearance is also similar to that of Britain's house elf, the brownie. The nymphs of Greek myths have many fairylike qualities. Though they always look young and beautiful, nymphs are believed to live ten thousand times longer than humans.

Origins of Native American Little People
Native Americans from throughout North and South America also worship many different deities connected with the different elements of nature. In Native American

mythology, not only do these nature spirits watch over the natural world, they are responsible for creating much of it.

According to several legends, the little people are as old as the earth itself. Legends from Mexico's Mayan culture contend little people are responsible for building the great temples and pyramids of the Yucatan peninsula. Other tales claim that the little people are rain spirits. According to an Aztec legend, as helpers of the rain god Tlaloc, the little people were there when lightning struck Food Mountain, releasing corn and beans for humans to eat.

In most Native American lore, the little people are supernatural assistants to humans, helping them find and grow food. Native American cultures respected the little people and their powers, and tribal mythology reflects that respect.

Christianity and the Fairies

Christian explanations for the existence of small magical beings tends to diminish the power and importance of these nature spirits. The Christian belief in one all-powerful God opposes the pagan belief in many gods and goddesses. Instead of completely denying the existence of those minor pagan deities, early Christian priests offered their own myths of fairy nature and origins. While changed by Christianity, fairies were never considered fully adopted into the host of heavenly beings. "Between good and evil, the archangel and the devil, legend discovers one being. This being is the Faerie. Between the paradise of Eden and the depths of hell, legend dreams of a world. This world is inhabited by Faeries,"[22] wrote Dubois in *The Great Encyclopedia of Faeries.*

Over time, people in Ireland and Scotland came to believe fairies were among the fallen angels in the biblical story of the heavenly battle between good and evil. The fairies were not considered to be followers of the devil, but rather his dupes. "When God made celestial beings choose between good and evil, between His kingdom and Satan's, those who did not come to a decision were separated from the angels and the demons to live in a gray limbo,"[23] wrote Dubois.

According to the Christian mythology of the British Isles, when the archangel Michael hurled Satan and his hosts out of Heaven, many smaller, more insignificant spirits fell out with them. God then closed the heavenly gates to save other angels from falling, thus stranding the small fairies outside. When the gates closed, the fairies stopped in their tracks and remained where they had landed, some in the sky, some in the mountains and woods, some in the sea, and some under the earth's surface. In this explanation, fairies are not condemned to evil but are not saved from it

A fifteenth-century painting shows the archangel Michael casting Satan and his servants out of Heaven. According to the Christian mythology of the British Isles, fairies fell to Earth with them.

either. "This is why on the day of the Last Judgment Faeries will not be raised from the dead, but will gently fade away like a luminous cloud,"[24] wrote Dubois. That cloud over the fairies' fate adds to their mystical nature, which has not yet begun to fade. The changing world of legend and mythology continues to make fairies mysterious and fascinating.

A different Christian explanation for fairy origins developed in Scandinavia where people often refer to the fairies as the *huldre*, or the hidden people. The Scandinavian tales offer a reason why fairies are invisible. One legend claims that the fairies descended from the hidden children of Eve. After Adam and Eve were expelled from the Garden of Eden, they settled down to domestic life and became the parents of many children. They had so many that Eve was ashamed. One day while visiting Earth, God called Eve and asked her to present her children to him. Eve sent half of the children to hide and brought out only the most presentable. God, however, was not fooled. In Katherine Briggs's account of the story, God declares, "Let those who were hidden from me, be hidden from all mankind."[25] Another Scandinavian tale about the *huldre* claims that the fairies were the offspring of Adam and his first wife, Lilith. Both versions of fairy origins suggest the *huldre* were half-human and half-mystical spirits like the angels.

Fairies of Fairy Tales

Many people's perceptions of fairies and fairy magic come from fairy tales. The most familiar fairy tales are so old it is difficult to determine their origins. What is known is that for generations people told the tales to entertain themselves. In the telling, they expressed local superstitions and customs.

The fairy godmother is an essential element of many well-known fairy tales. Different versions of the fairy god-

The Tooth Fairy

Just before going to bed, children put their loose baby teeth under their pillows in hopes of finding money in their place in the morning. The magic supposedly is the work of the tooth fairy. The origins of the tooth fairy predate Christianity. The tooth fairy evolved from the old crones of pagan religions. In pagan times, people believed witches or evil fairies could cast spells on children whose hairclippings or loose teeth they acquired. Eventually people came to believe keeping baby teeth and a lock of baby hair would protect them from evil throughout their lives. In Victorian times, many people had elaborately embroidered lace pillows with special pockets for keeping baby teeth safe.

Today, the tooth fairy is so popular that a Chicago dentist opened a tooth fairy museum in her home. Called the Tooth Fairy Consultant, the museum has about six hundred visitors a year. Museum founder Dr. Rosemary Wells was quoted in Cassandra Eason's book, *A Complete Guide to Faeries and Magical Beings*, as saying, "Other fairies are just cute but the Tooth Fairy has a specific purpose, helping children get through a tough time."

The modern tooth fairy is a relic of pagan folklore.

mother exist throughout European mythology. In all forms, fairy godmothers watch over a newborn, bestowing special gifts upon the infant. In Albania, the Fatis present an infant with gifts the third day after birth. In Wales, they are called good mothers. In eastern Europe, the Laume are thought to preside over the births, marriages, and deaths of humans.

Many people believe fairy godmothers developed from the Fates of Greek mythology. The Greek Fates are the three women who spin, measure, and cut the thread of mortals' destinies. Others believe fairy godmothers descended from the triple Matres of Celtic mythology. The Matres watch over people and their homes. In one French version of the fairy tale Cinderella, the fairy godmother is portrayed as being the Virgin Mary.

Fairy tales are full of fairy godmothers who give gifts and protect children or young girls from the curses of bad fairies. In this respect, the fairy godmother is often associated with wisdom and farsightedness. Today's godmothers are not of the fairy race but rather they are loving friends or relatives who have taken on the responsibility of watching over a child from birth to adulthood.

The magic in fairy tales is often attributed to fairies and associated with secrecy. The priests of ancient pagan religions, from which many myths concerning fairies originate, kept their knowledge secret. Many people believe each fairy has a secret name—the fairy's real name. These real names reveal the fairy's real nature. Most fairies judiciously guard their secret names and natures from humans. According to superstition, knowing a fairy's real name can be both hazardous and rewarding. One fairy might grant wishes or give magical powers to those who discover its secret. Another fairy might curse the person who says its real name. Sometimes fairies will use their secret name as a tool to bargain with humans, as in the well-known fairy tale Rumpelstiltskin.

What people believe about fairies originates from ancient religions, myths, superstitions, and fairy tales. The many beliefs about these magical beings make up an ever-changing perception of fairy power and influence known as the fairy faith.

Chapter 3

The Evolution of the Fairy Faith

Fairy faith can simply mean believing that fairies exist, believing in superstitions concerning fairies, or believing in the spirits and practices of modern versions of ancient pagan religions. Fairy faith has survived in many different forms for thousands of years. When fairy faith was most influential, it attributed great power to its magical spirits, the fairies.

Fairies have gained and lost powers as the cultures embracing fairy faith have changed and developed. People's beliefs about fairies change almost as much as the fairies themselves change. People have thought of fairies as child-like beings whose sole purpose is to beautify a garden like the fairy character in William Shakespeare's *A Midsummer Night's Dream* who says:

> I must seek some dewdrops here,
> And hang a pearl in every cowslip's ear.[26]

People have also thought of fairies as strong spirits with the capacity for doing great good or great evil. Stories of the most powerful fairies developed from ancient pagan societies.

Fairies and Ancient Celtic Faith

Long before the ancient Romans invaded Britain in the first century B.C., Celtic priests and priestesses ruled the British Isles. This priestly class included the teachers, healers, prophets, and leaders of ancient Celtic communities. The Celts' beliefs differed slightly from community to community. While most Celts performed similar religious rituals and practices, different tribes or clans had their own deities. For example, Brigid, the goddess of wisdom, was the most important and powerful deity for the Brigantes in Ireland. Elsewhere in ancient Britain other gods would be favored. The local gods and goddesses became the fairies of

Celtic priests served as leaders and teachers of their people. The Celts believed that fairies shared their wisdom with these priests.

the mythology of the British Isles and an integral part of the fairy faith in individual communities.

The Celtic priests and priestesses kept secret the knowledge they gained from nature and the fairies. Nothing was written down; the priests memorized all the magic spells, poetry, and knowledge of nature and passed this information on orally to their successors. This knowledge included an understanding of the healing power of certain plants and herbs like mistletoe and a knowledge of the stars and astronomy and the science of physics.

By keeping their knowledge secret from the other clan members, Celtic priests and priestesses maintained control over their society. The stories of powerful fairies, told by ruling priests, presented and reinforced the values of individual communities while helping the priestly class keep control over the people. That control would be challenged by invading Romans.

Fairies and the Roman Influence

The Roman emperor Julius Caesar invaded the British Isles in 55 B.C. The Romans built roads, aqueducts, and fortresses in Britain. They also brought Roman ideas, culture, and religion to the Celtic people.

The Roman religion resembled ancient Celtic beliefs. Even Julius Caesar, in his writings about his military campaigns, recognized the similarities between Roman and Celtic religions. Caesar wrote of the Celts' beliefs, "As one of their leading dogmas, they include this: that souls are not annihilated, but pass after death from one body to another, and they hold that by this teaching, men are much encouraged to valor, through disregarding the fear of death."[27]

Roman invaders were also impressed with Celtic culture and the knowledge of their pagan priests. Caesar took note of the learning displayed by Celtic leaders, stating, "They also discuss and impart to their young many things concerning the heavenly bodies and their movements, the size of the world and our earth, natural sciences, and the influence and power of the immortal gods."[28]

The similarities between the Roman and Celtic religions helped them both blend and coincide with each other under Roman rule of the British Isles. Although Roman law forbade many Celtic religious practices and many priests and priestesses lost their place as leaders of Celtic society, the beliefs of the Celts in their gods and the fairies remained. It was not until near the end of the Roman Empire, when Christianity became the predominant religion across Europe and in the British Isles, that fairy powers and fairy origins changed.

Christian Conversion

In medieval times, Christian priests and monks worked hard to discredit pagan religious practices. Anything pagan was considered evil and feared, which included Celtic gods and the fairies. Ireland's Saint Patrick was known to pray to God for protection against the incantations of pagan priests.

Still, the peasants of the British Isles could not quickly or easily give up rituals and traditions practiced over centuries. According to John Matthews in *The Druid Source Book*, "While they might be baptized into Christianity—few peasants [farmers or builders] like to put a spade into a so-called 'Dane's fort' [fairy habitat] for fear of the wrath of the 'good people' [the fairies]."[29] Christian leaders soon found it was easier to incorporate pagan practices and idols into their religion than to obliterate them. Christian priests would bless pagan idols presented to them, making them "Christian." The idols could then be left with the pagan "converts." The Christian priesthood also worked to convert nonbelievers.

Eventually many pagan gods and goddesses, including powerful fairies, were assimilated into Christian culture. Some became ghosts or demons, others legendary heroes and heroines. Some pagan spirits were transformed by Christian storytellers, who crafted what became known as transition stories. One of these tales was about the lovely fairy Ethne. Ethne was a member of Manannan mac Lir, an Irish fairy court. While bathing, Ethne lost her veil of invisibility. Wandering into a monastery garden, she met monks who received her into the church. She then converted to Christianity. But there came a time when her Christian prayers were distracted by soft, sad voices from her past life calling her name. The confusion in her heart was too great for Ethne, and she ended up dying in the arms of Saint Patrick.

Patrick was not the only Christian saint to deal with the remnants of pagan faiths. Saint Brendan is believed to have converted several fairies to Christianity. Saint Brendan was often referred to as Brendan the Navigator because many believed he led sixty monks on a voyage across the Atlantic

Saint Patrick drives the snakes from Ireland in this illustration of the popular story. Patrick held that all pagan beliefs, including the belief in fairies, were evil.

Ocean in search of the Land of Promise. Legend has it that on this journey he encountered many supernatural beings including a group of mermaids. Saint Brendan is believed to have converted the mermaids to Christianity.

Saint Brendan's converts were not the only mermaids to accept Christianity. One legend tells of a mermaid who was not only baptized a Christian but became a saint. She was called Murgen, which means "sea born," and she was believed to have had an unusual past. Allegedly, three hundred years before her death in the sixth century, Murgen had been a little girl named Liban whose family died in a flood off the shores of Belfast Lough in northern Ireland. After the floodwaters overtook them, Murgen supposedly managed to live beneath the waves. Gradually she became a mermaid. According to the legend, one day, men rowing a boat upon the lake heard Murgen singing. Following her songs, the men managed to catch her in a net. Later they displayed her in a tank of water for everyone to see. She was baptized there, and by the time she died, many miracles were attributed to her. She was later admitted into some of the old Catholic calendars as Saint Murgen.

Fairies and the Arthurian Legend

Nowhere does Christianity, history, and fairy lore meet so powerfully as in the legend of King Arthur and the Knights of the Round Table. The story went through several transformations over the centuries, and those revisions reveal changes in religious, political, and historical beliefs—and in beliefs about fairies. Figures of the fairy faith, like the wizard Merlin, the sorceress Morgan le Fay, and Viviene (the water spirit known as the Lady of the Lake), were part of a legend that combined pagan beliefs with early Christianity.

Historically, the real Arthur was probably a Romanized Britain who helped unite clans to fight northern invaders around A.D. 150. The earliest versions of the legend are simply about a warrior king; pagan spirits and Christian icons were later added. The most familiar version of the Arthurian legend is that of an orphan who rises to power after being trained in the fairy faith by the wizard Merlin. With help from the Knights of the Round Table, King Arthur rules the British Isles from his royal court at Camelot. Female fairies play prominently in the tale both by helping and hurting the hero, Arthur. Viviene, the Lady of the Lake, gives Arthur Excalibur, a magical sword that protects him in battle. Arthur's half-sister Morgan le Fay, queen of the fairy kingdom Avalon, successfully plots the downfall of her brother and Camelot.

Viviene judges King Arthur worthy to receive Excalibur. Some scholars believe that the character of Viviene evolved from stories of ancient Celtic water fairies.

Historical researcher David Day believes the characters of Morgan le Fay and Viviene originated from tales of the White Ladies, old Celtic water deities who were found in sacred fountains, lakes, and rivers. Some Irish water fairies are still referred to as Morgans today. Day contends Morgan was not always portrayed as an evil fairy but as a mystic and healer. She first appeared in Geoffrey of Monmouth's *Life of Merlin*, written in the early half of the twelfth century. In Monmouth's version, Morgan led nine holy women from Avalon to tend Arthur's wounds after Camelot fell to evil forces. In this story, Morgan was not related to Arthur but she fell in love with him. In turn, the king agreed to stay with Morgan le Fay in Avalon. By the end of the twelfth century, authors of Arthurian Romances proclaimed Morgan to be Arthur's sister but she remained an ally. Within the next one hundred years, Morgan became totally evil.

Morgan le Fay's transformation from good to bad was due to the writings of the Cistercian monks sometime between 1230 and 1250. The Cistercians were not placid students of Christian scripture. They were fierce warriors who swore to exterminate all infidels and heretics, including those of the fairy faith. The scribes of this group rewrote literature to portray anything sexual or female as bad. In his book *The Search for King Arthur*, David Day wrote, "The Cistercians believed that it was blasphemous to attribute healing or prophetic powers to a female who was not a member of a religious order and, furthermore, that such powers undermined the authority of the priesthood and the church."[30] In reinterpreting the Arthurian legend, the Cistercians portrayed Morgan le Fay as possessed by demons and adulterous. Instead of being a healing lover, she is depicted as a rival sibling who has had an incestuous relationship with her half-brother Arthur.

While Morgan le Fay never fully regained her once-positive status, the fairy faith eventually regained acceptance. In the 1500s, women and fairies would once again be embraced by the people of the British Isles when Elizabeth I, also known as the Faerie Queen, came to power.

Fairy Acceptance in the Elizabethan Age

The popularization of the word *fairy* came during a period of renewed interest in British culture. Before that time, most people referred to those beings of Celtic mythology as

Fairies were a very popular subject of British literature during the reign of Queen Elizabeth I. Many practiced the fairy faith during this era.

elves. *Fairy*, a decidedly more feminine term, replaced *elf* during the reign of one of England's most powerful monarchs, Elizabeth I, who ruled England and Ireland from 1558 to 1603.

Under Queen Elizabeth, Britain also experienced a resurgence in the practice of the fairy faith. In fact, the beginning of the Elizabethan Age was determined from the calculations of a practitioner of the faith. Welshman John Dee, a prophet and astrologer trained in ancient Celtic rituals, set the date for Elizabeth's coronation. Many believe

Dee was the inspiration for the magician and mystic Prospero, the main character in Elizabethan playwright William Shakespeare's play *The Tempest*.

By the Elizabethan Age, the church no longer had a strong influence on society in the British Isles—this was partly due to the reign of Elizabeth's father, King Henry VIII. Henry had broken away from the Catholic Church, which forbade divorce, and established the Church of England so he could leave his wife to marry Elizabeth's mother, Anne Boleyn. Elizabeth proved to be as strong and as independent a leader as her father. During her reign, she built up a powerful naval force, encouraged colonization of the New World, and established England as a major European power. Culture, art, and especially literature thrived under Elizabeth's leadership. Celtic mythology—primarily stories about fairies—once again became a popular source for poems and plays. Edmund Spenser wrote his epic poem "The Faerie Queen" and dedicated it to Queen Elizabeth. One of the most complex and entertaining plays about fairy life was also written during this period, Shakespeare's *A Midsummer Night's Dream*.

In the two centuries following Elizabeth's reign, the fairy faith faded away into the realm of myth and fantasy. Beyond the political connections of the various versions of the Arthurian legends, fairies have long been a source of inspiration for classic and modern literature. These fairy stories also provide some insight into views of good and evil, women's role in society, and the power of fairy faith.

Literature and Fairy Faith

Fairies are believed to provoke the imagination and to inspire artists of all kinds to produce great works. Some believe literature could not be written without inspiration from the fairies. In *The Enchanted Garden*, Claire O'Rush writes, "Creative works of literature which penetrate the mysteries of life are not written without the granting of fairy insights."[31] Writers of literature in particular are drawn to unraveling the complex and mystical nature of fairies.

Some people believe fairies are interesting because they exhibit all the foibles and failings of human beings while maintaining supernatural powers. In Shakespeare's *A Midsummer Night's Dream*, fairy characters, fairy lore, and fairy magic come together to create a farce. The play is about England's flower fairies. While most people think flower fairies do little more than tend to blossoms, Shakespeare's characters have powers to ruin crops, foul up the seasons, and make people fall in love. While exhibiting humanlike emotions, these flower fairies fall prey to many foolish pranks. Much of the humor in the play stems from how the social structure of this fairy monarchy can be undone by the lowly Puck, a fairy who resembles a court jester in character. At the end of the play, order is restored from comic chaos and Puck proclaims,

A scene from William Shakespeare's A Midsummer Night's Dream. *Mischievous flower fairies create comedic havoc in the play.*

> If we shadows have offended,
> Think but this, and all is
>   mended, . . .
> And this weak and idle theme,
> No more yielding but a dream.[32]

Other more serious plots suggest fairies are capable of great evil. In 1782, German poet and novelist Johann Wolfgang von Goethe made famous the tale of the evil Elf King who abducts human children. Goethe's *Erlkonig* is the story of a small boy riding through a snowstorm with his father. In a 1955 English translation, the boy sees the Elf King, who approaches him, saying:

> Sweet lad, o come and join me do!
> Such pretty games I will play with you;
> On the shore gay flowers the colours unfold
> My mother has many garments of gold.
> Will you, sweet lad, come along with me?[33]

The boy refuses and tells his father about his vision. At first the father does not believe his son's claim, but once the boy says the Elf King hurt him, the father fears for the boy's life. He takes his son and hurries home. When he arrives, the father discovers that his boy has died. The Elf King's sweet temptations have turned to vengeance against the boy's refusal to come away with him.

Bram Stoker's *Dracula*, published in 1897, was inspired by equally frightening fairy stories the author's mother told him during his childhood. Stoker heard stories like those about Scottish *glaistigs* which are evil female fairies exhibiting vampire-like characteristics. The *glaistigs* were believed to kill cattle and their human owners. While appearing friendly, the *glaistigs* would think nothing of slashing the throats of hunters to drink their blood or appearing as a man's loved one only to suck his veins dry. The belief and fear of the *glaistigs* were so strong that even into the 1890s many people tried to appease these evil fairies with offerings of fresh milk. The stories about *glaistigs* appear to promote the idea that female power and sexuality are dangerous and can destroy men. Although the evil in Stoker's book comes primarily from the male vampire, Count Dracula, his characteristics are the same as the *glaistigs*.

Fairies became more positive in nature when much of their power was taken away. Most Victorian literature portrays fairies as quaint companions of children. In J.M. Barrie's play *Peter Pan*, first produced in the early 1900s, the fairy Tinkerbell needs children to believe in her to stay alive. The children in the audience save Tinkerbell simply by clapping. Barrie's plot implies that the fairies' supernatural powers are not even as potent as children's imaginations.

Revival in the Victorian Era

Several developments from the mid-1800s to the early 1900s helped to increase Britain's fascination with its fairies. One had to do with the reign of a very popular monarch, Queen Victoria. Victoria ruled Britain and Ireland from 1837 until her death in 1901. During her long reign, Britain experienced a new sense of national pride and a revived interest in all things British, including English literature, legends, and fairy lore. However, the days of thinking of fairies as gods and goddesses of nature were over. Fairies were reduced from powerful spirits to benign beings of children's imaginations.

Childhood became recognized as an important developmental stage of human life and such things related to children—stories, toys, and games—became more popular. One reason for this might be that industrial and technological advances allowed parents and children to spend more time together. It seemed Queen Victoria and her husband, Prince Albert, also influenced this new feeling about children and childhood. Children and family were certainly important to the royal couple—they were the parents of nine. During the Victorian era, fairy tales were written primarily for and told to children. It was not long before a common notion developed that children, being more sensitive to fairies, were the only human beings able to see the tiny spirits.

Other theories concerning the existence of fairies also emerged during this time. Two religious philosophies, Spiritualism and Theosophy, became popular in the Victorian era. Both stressed the existence of unseen spirits

During the reign of Queen Victoria, depicted kneeling at her coronation, fairy tales were extremely popular. Many Victorians believed that only children could see fairies.

such as angels, ghosts, and fairies. Neither, however, attributed much power or influence to the fairies. While Theosophists believed fairies inhabited a higher spiritual dimension than most human beings, fairy influence did not go beyond inspiring poets or artists. Spiritualists focused on making contact with the dead. To them, fairies were little more than invisible nuisances who occasionally interrupted séances.

The art and literature of the Victorian era portrayed fairies as tiny spirits mostly protecting and presiding over flower gardens. Fairies became lovely yet insignificant spirits encountered only by children and a few adults.

Necessary Part of Daily Life

Across the Atlantic, in the United States, Native Americans respected (and continue to respect) the little people as influential nature spirits. Native American little people are considered friendly toward humans and in many cases necessary allies for daily life. "From the little people come rain and wind. From their cooking pots comes food that never runs out. They themselves are small, but their strength and wisdom are great,"[34] writes John Bierhorst in his book *The Deetkatoo: Native American Stories about Little People.*

Native Americans believe that the little people are a source of power, and they often ask these spirits for help in a special way. According to Bierhorst: "One in need would identify with the little helper, using the words 'I am to fail in nothing! I am a Little Man.' Or seeking protection, the user could call out to the helper, 'You will be holding my soul in your clenched hand!'"[35] Even some Cherokee doctors today have been known to call upon the little people to help them cure the sick.

Native Americans are rarely surprised by encountering a little person. In fact, in many Native American cultures, little people are just a part of everyday life. A young Cherokee woman from North Carolina describes hearing a little person as a very commonplace experience: "My mom's boyfriend says that his house is protected by the little people. One evening I was there by myself, and I could hear [the little person's] footsteps back in the hall."[36]

The Fairy Faith Today

Today, Celtic art, music, myth, and magic are more popular than ever. This growing interest in everything Celtic includes a revival of the fairy faith. More and more people in the British Isles are beginning to connect the fairies with the powers of nature and their ancient Celtic roots. For many modern practitioners of the fairy faith, the ancient Celtic religions offer a way to recover nature's lost resources and beauty. "Earth is now badly scarred because of our greed and ignorance. But perhaps there is a way of . . .

healing the planet, ourselves and others through the creation of our own enchanted garden,"[37] wrote Claire O'Rush in her book *The Enchanted Garden.*

Some fairy faith believers find truth in the Celtic myths—from the tales of fairy gods and goddesses to the ever-changing legend of King Arthur to the reports of human and fairy encounters. Often Christian and ancient Celtic beliefs are combined with modern meditation practices to create a new form of worship. The new versions of ancient Celtic tradition encourage meditation as a way to enter the fairy realm and receive mystical guidance in difficult times. Celtic scholar Steve Blamires, author of *Glamoury: Magic of the Celtic Green World,* believes "Celtic tradition is the acceptance of personal responsibility and realization that all of us constantly shape and affect the

Puritans and the Fairies

Unlike Catholic priests, who opted to combine and convert pagan beliefs with Christianity, Puritan ministers condemned all pagan idols and practices as evil or heathen. This attitude did not win the Puritans many converts. Many people from Scotland voiced their resentment against Puritan ministers in the late 1800s. In *The Vanishing People*, folklorist Katherine Briggs quotes a Scotsman named Angus MacLeod who was tired of Puritan clerics telling him that fairy stories, fairy music, and fairy dances were evil.

MacLeod recalled how his mother said she had seen fairies dancing on a knoll. He said she described the fairies as: "[Having skin] as white as the swan of the wave, and their voice was as melodious as the mavis of the wood, and they themselves were as beauteous of feature and as lithe of form as a picture." MacLeod loved the

tales his mother told him of the fairies. As a child, he remembered his mother showing him how the fairies danced. "If there were quarrels among children, as there were, and as there will be, my beloved mother would set us to dance there and then. We would dance there till we were seven times tired. A stream of sweat would be falling from us before we stopped."

The Puritan ministers' proclamations did not change MacLeod's mind about the fairies. However, MacLeod believed the ministers' teaching eventually banished the fairies from the Scottish countryside. This angered MacLeod. "May ill befall them! And what have the clerics put in their place? Beliefs about creeds, and disputations about denominations and churches!" said MacLeod about the ministers. "The black clerics have suppressed every noble custom among the people of the Gaeldom."

land on which we live." According to Blamires, part of this view includes the interrelationship between the fairy realm and the human world. "The Celtic world view is a magical one, in which everything has a physical, mental, and spiritual aspect and its own proper purpose, and where our every act affects both worlds."[38]

But even fairy faith practitioners and Celtic scholars like Blamires admit fairies remain unpredictable. "There are also as many deceivers and tricksters in the Otherworld [the fairy realm] as there are in this world, as the legends reveal. You should be as wary and cautious while journeying in the Otherworld as you would be when journeying within unknown land of this world."[39] This growing belief in fairies and fairy faith is built upon that unpredictability and the long history of human encounters with these mystical beings.

Chapter 4

Human Encounters with Fairies

Superstitions in the British Isles often warn of fairy entanglements. Many elderly men and women in Ireland, Scotland, and Wales take those superstitions seriously. As reported in Ward Rutherford's book *Celtic Lore*, one angry old man chased away local archaeologists at a dig near Jersey, England, in 1912. Waving his cane in the air, he yelled, "If you disturb the fairies you will bring trouble on the neighborhood."[40] Later, workmen refused to dig on or near that same spot. Even those who seek out meetings with fairies believe they must do so with caution because fairies are so unpredictable.

Fairy Communication

Communication with mystical spirits like the fairies differs from communication with people. Most people would not recognize what some claim are messages from the fairies.

Many artists and writers believe fairies are the source of their inspiration. According to artist and writer Brian Froud, invisible fairies populate his studio and "snooze among the books and paints, flit through the windows, nest in the cupbords, play silly pranks, and offer bright gifts."[41] Froud believes the tricks the fairies play make him see things from a new perspective. "My paintings [of fairies] are not illustrations drawn from specific stories or folklore texts; rather, they are images painted intuitively, springing directly from visions guided by faery muses, a paradoxical mix of chance and intent,"[42] wrote Froud in his book *Good Faeries, Bad Faeries.*

Claire O'Rush is a descendant from a long line of wise-women from Yorkshire, England, as well as an author. Wisewomen understand the fairy faith as it concerns nature and the fairies. O'Rush believes the ability to see and communicate with fairies often develops through the contemplation of art, the reading of poetry, and the possession of a free imagination. O'Rush's great-great-grandmother, a Victorian wisewoman named Sarah Greaves, wrote that the marvels of nature and the garden help to bring people closer to the fairies. "You must nurture feelings of wonder, reverence and love for every detail of your garden," wrote Greaves. "The moon and the stars which silently look down on it, the great sun which is the source of its being and for the clouds and the changing skies which provide it with a canopy. When you can truly feel the sweetness of this magic, you will begin to discover the fairies."[43]

Watching Fairies

Often children claim to find fairies while gazing at flowers or trees. According to many accounts, it seems as if the fairies are teaching these young humans about the unseen mysteries of nature. In the late 1980s, Cassandra Eason, author of *A Complete Guide to Faeries and Magical Beings*, interviewed several people who claimed to have seen fairies when they were children. Many of these sightings occurred around gardens and backyard trees. A woman named Lilian said, "I used to see fairies in our garden in Cheshire, but especially in the woods. They were semi-transparent and tiny with wings. I found myself looking at the little people in shadowing forms. They all looked different according to whether they belonged to a tree, a flower or a bush. I knew I was only a visitor—watching, not part. I never told the other children. I knew they would jeer."[44] A few others told Eason that they recalled seeing fairies while looking out the windows of their childhood bedrooms. Dr. David Lewis of Shrewsbury in Shropshire, England, remembered looking out his uncurtained bay window at

A tiny fairy reaches up to light a lamp in the form of a flower. Many fairy sightings occur in gardens or among trees.

night and seeing beings that looked like colorful birds. "They were luminous creatures about the size of birds which moved occasionally through the branches," Lewis said. "When they moved they left a trail of light, which soon faded."[45]

Some people consider finding or losing an unusual object to be an encounter with a fairy. In her book *Green Witchcraft: Folk Magic, Fairy Lore and Herb Craft*, Ann Moura writes about her daughter finding a small stone teacup. "I told her to keep it safe as it was a fairy cup, and she did for many years," Moura recalled. "One day the cup simply disappeared from her room and she was very upset about it. I told her the fairies must have wanted it back and would probably leave something else for her."[46] Later, Moura's daughter found a pretty, engraved golden ring that fit her perfectly.

Communicating with the fairies through lost and found objects and creative inspiration lacks the hard evidence that human senses provide. While many people think seeing is believing, most stories or personal accounts of human meetings with fairies begin with hearing enchanted music.

The Lure of Fairy Music

In the early 1900s, folklore researchers roaming the Irish, Scottish, and Welsh countrysides talked to local residents about their beliefs. It was easy for the folklorists to find elderly men and women anxious to share their own experiences with the fairies. Few claimed to have seen fairies but many said they heard their music. "I heard the pipes there in that wood," said seventy-year-old John, pointing to a wood on the northwest slope of a hill in Ireland. "I heard the music another time on a summer evening at the Rath of Ringlestown, in a field where all the grass has been burned off—it is the grandest kind of music. It may last half the night, but once day comes, it ends."[47]

However beautiful the melody, most people who believe in fairies are wary of fairy music. Fairy music is believed to enchant the listener, and few who claimed to have heard it are left unchanged by the experience.

Playing violins, singing, and dancing are common nightly activities for fairies. Their music is believed to lure people into their world. Often fairies sing and dance in fairy rings, circles of toadstools that serve as arenas for fairy revelry. Superstition declares stepping into a fairy ring can be hazardous—some people find themselves captured by the fairies and others are bewitched to join in the dance. A friend can save someone who is trapped in a dancing frenzy of a fairy ring. By keeping one foot firmly outside the ring

An illustration depicts a fairy playing a flute during a full moon. Fairy music enchants and lures the listener into fairyland.

and reaching in, grabbing the victim's coattails, the bewitched dancer can be pulled out of the ring. Avoiding the ring altogether is always wise. But sometimes the lure of the music is too great, as in the Irish tale of Tudur of Llangollen. When Tudur came upon a fairy ring he tried to resist joining in the revelry, but eventually it was too much for him. He shouted at the fairy fiddler to play and he began to dance. Suddenly, the fiddler sprouted horns and a tail, the other fairies turned into animals, and Tudur's dance grew wilder. Tudur was found the following day dancing alone like a madman. The recitation of some Bible verses broke the fairies' spell and Tudur returned to his home a wiser man.

Occasionally, fairies have been thought to bless the listener, as in the case of the tale of Lusmore the Hunchback, which Katherine Briggs gives an account of in her book *The Vanishing People.* Feeling the full weight of the hump growing on his back, Lusmore passed by a group of singing fairies. They sang, "Monday! Tuesday!" and then paused. The melody was lovely but the lyrics lacked something. At the pause, Lusmore quickly chimed in, "and Wednesday too!" Appreciating Lusmore's addition to their song, the fairies recited the spell:

Lusmore! Lusmore!
Doubt not nor deplore,
For the hump which you bore
On your back is no more.
Look down on the floor,
And view it, Lusmore![48]

Lusmore, no longer a hunchback, stood up straight, thanked the fairies, and went home happy.

According to many legends, fairy music can sound so sweet and alluring it can totally enchant the listener, drawing the person deep into the realm of fairyland. The Irish tale of the voyage of Bran tells of such a capture. Bran was lured by a strange and lovely song to visit the enchanted Isle of Women. There he met a fairy queen whom he chose to live with, never to return to the mortal world.

Most people who believe in fairies avoid mystical melodies and the haunting lyrics because they are afraid of becoming fairy captives. For those who have already entered the fairy realm, it is best to avoid all fairy food or water for superstition dictates tasting anything from the fairies will trap a mortal in their enchanted world. These captured mortals are then unable to return to their human lives. Those few lucky enough to return from the realm of the fairies often come back possessing gifts they never had before.

Fairy Gifts

The folklore of the British Isles is full of accounts of fairies bestowing special powers and talents on a few special people. The most famous of these is the story of Thomas the Rhymer, who many consider to be Scotland's national prophet. Thomas was a real person who lived in the thirteenth century. He gained fame when his prophecies and poetry were published roughly two hundred years later. What made Thomas the Rhymer's story fascinating was that he claimed the fairies gave him the gifts of poetry and prophecy.

According to legend, while lying under his favorite tree, a young Thomas saw the queen of the fairies who lived in Eildon Hills. A poem attributed to Thomas the Rhymer describes the fairy queen.

> Her skirt was of the grass green silk,
> Her mantle of the velvet fine
> At each tett of her horse's mane
> Hung fifty silver bells and nine,
> All hail, thou mighty Queen of Heaven
> For thy peer on earth I never did see.[49]

Instantly enchanted, Thomas fell in love with the beautiful queen and agreed to accompany her to her fairy realm. Thomas lived there with the fairy queen for seven years. Thomas returned to his mortal home wearing green and carrying a special harp, which gave Thomas the ability to write and perform beautiful songs.

Thomas the Rhymer never spoke of his time with the fairies but he was able to foretell the future as well as understand the mysteries of the past. Thomas told tales of King Arthur and Merlin the Magician in epic ballads. He also accurately predicted many significant events in Great

Britain's history, including the uniting of Scotland and England. Thomas the Rhymer lived to be an old man and many believe that when he died he went back to fairyland to be with his fairy queen.

Butterflies draw a fairy queen in an airborne carriage. Fairy queens are described as beings of incomparable beauty.

An English servant named Anne Jefferies claimed to have had a similar experience with the fairies in 1645 when she was nineteen years old. She was sitting and knitting in her mistress's garden when she caught sight of six small fairies all dressed in green. Frightened, she screamed and went into a kind of convulsion which left her paralyzed for a short time. When she finally recovered, she was able to perform miracles such as curing her mistress's leg, which had been hurt in a fall.

Blaming Fairies

While people claimed to have benefited from encounters with fairies, most superstitions prevalent in the British Isles warn of such meetings. Many blame fairies for the unimaginable and unexplainable misfortunes that happen to them. Fairies have long been blamed for illnesses, sleeping problems, and even acne. For many people, fairies serve as explanations for why things go wrong.

Superstitions claim the slightest contact with the fairies will cause humans harm. A fairy's glance can make a person forgetful. Angry fairies can blind humans by spitting in their eyes. Many people believe evil or just plain mischievous fairies are responsible for human deformities, barrenness, backaches, and sneezes. According to folklorist Katherine Briggs, people who wake up tired are believed to have been lured in their sleep to nightly fairy dances or bewitched to work all night for the fairies.

Dancing for the West African Bori

The Hausa of West Africa believe fairies called the Bori are responsible for every sickness or misfortune known to mankind. Each individual Bori causes a specific illness or problem. The power of the Bori to harm the Hausa can be dispelled through individual dances and specific songs. While dancing and singing, the Hausa actually are inviting the Bori fairies to join in the festivities and thus appease them. The Hausa usually perform for 150 Bori guests during these rituals.

There are times when the Bori are useful to humans, as when people are building new homes or starting new businesses. But each Bori asked to help in these endeavors must be thanked with specific sacrifices. Some Bori require simple offerings of food or game for their favors; others prefer songs or paintings. If a Bori becomes offended, it will kill the offender by slowly sucking away the person's life force in a method similar to the vampires of European mythology.

The Hausa people of West Africa believe that their well-being depends on the will of fairies known as Bori.

"Fairy stroke" and "touched by the fairies" are expressions refering to all kinds of adverse conditions. Commonly used in the British Isles, these two phrases denote at least two ways in which fairies inflict disease and disaster upon human beings. Some believe a fairy stroke is caused by elves shooting people with tiny flint arrows. Brian Froud offers another cause for fairy strokes in his book *Good Faeries, Bad Faeries*. He believes the malady is caused by "invisible fairy fingers stroking their victims into seizures."[50] However fairy strokes are believed to be caused, they are blamed for a multitude of physical ailments including paralysis, lameness of limbs, comas, and tuberculosis. "Touched by the fairies" can refer to an unexplained loss of sanity, or simply to overwhelming problems that arise unexpectedly.

Despite the potential illness or misfortune arising from fairy encounters, there are cures for fairy mischief. Ripping a shirt, washing in a south-running stream, gathering moss from the water of a millstream, pouring salt on a table, and saying the Lord's Prayer three times are all thought of as ways to break fairy curses. But perhaps the worst problems blamed upon the fairies are not fixed easily because they concern the early loss of children. There are many tales about fairy changelings and their effect upon human parents and children.

Fairy Changelings

Many people believed babies need to be baptized to protect them from the fairies. Ancient superstitions and legends warn of fairies stealing healthy human babies and replacing them with changelings. The extra-cautious believers might lay a crucifix or iron tongs across a baby's bed to keep the human infant from being replaced by a fairy changeling.

Fairy changelings can be fairy children, old fairies disguised as babies, or pieces of wood enchanted to appear as human infants. People might suspect a baby with a difficult

A fairy carrying a human baby flies into the woods. Fairies are believed to steal babies, replacing them with changelings.

temperament is actually a fairy changeling. Human babies are thought to be happy and pleasant, which is often the reason given for why fairies steal them. Bob Curran, author of *A Field Guide to Irish Fairies*, describes a changeling as "never happy, except when some calamity befalls the household. For the most part, it howls and screeches throughout its waking hours and the sound and frequency of its yells, often transcend the bounds of mortal endurance."[51]

Children believed to be changelings often suffer at the hands of superstitious parents. In 1843 in Penzance, England, J. Trevelyan and his wife were charged with mistreating one of their children. Evidence suggested the child was regularly beaten by both parents and their servants and forced to live outside when only fifteen months old. In court, the Trevelyans claimed the child was nothing but a changeling, and the case against them was immediately dismissed.

Changelings generally are believed to bring bad luck to a home. They eat too much and drain family finances, but they are also thought to bring enchanting music into their mortal homes. In his book, Curran quotes a man from County Fermanagh who claimed to encounter a musical changeling:

> I saw a changeling one time. He lived with two oul' brothers away beyond the Dog's Well and looked like a wee wizened monkey. He was about ten or eleven but he couldn't really walk, just bobbed about. But he could play the whistle the best that you ever heard. Old tunes that the people had long forgotten, that was all he played. Then one day, he was gone and I don't know what happened to him at all.[52]

Few changeling stories end happily. The fairy children usually die or vanish, leaving grieving mortal parents behind. Occasionally, the human baby will be returned in exchange for a well-cared-for changeling. One such story was told by Lady Wilde in her book *Ancient Legends of Ireland*. The fairy queen switched her son with a beautiful human baby. The mortal mother took such good care of the changeling that the fairy queen decided to take him back. Being grateful for the care bestowed upon her fairy child, the fairy queen delivered the human baby back to its mother. "Take him," said the Queen, "he is your own child, that we carried away for he was so beautiful; and the boy you have at home is mine, a little elfish imp. Still, I want him back, and I have sent a man to bring him here; and you may take your own lively child home in safety, for the fairy blessings are on him for good."[53]

Countless fairy tales have been written about changelings given to deserving human couples who are unable to have children of their own. In these stories, the changelings usually have happy childhoods with caring parents. There always comes a time though when these human-raised changelings must follow their destiny and return to the fairy realm. The human parents grieve the loss of their fairy children, but if they have been good parents they are blessed by the fairies for the rest of their lives.

Fairy Wives

Adult fairies are also thought to be able to join human families. Many people believe fairies can and do marry mortals. It is believed that many female fairies are beautiful and alluring enough that few human men can resist them. While some fairies are thought to become lovers of mortal men, others are thought to become their wives. Even today, several well-known Irish families such as the O'Flahertys and O'Sullivans of County Kerry and the MacNamaras of County Clare claim fairy wives as their ancestors.

The majority of stories about fairy wives involve water fairies such as mermaids, *selkies*, and *merrows*. In the late 1800s, the Irish poet W.B. Yeats wrote about one such claim in his book *Irish Fairy and Folk Tales*. "Near Bantry in the last century, there is said to have been a woman, covered in scales like a fish, who was descended from such a marriage."[54]

In some stories, fairies are not luring mortals but are tricked into marriage by human men. Tradition declares that Irish *merrows* have sealskin cloaks that allow them to live in the sea. They shed these cloaks when they come on land, usually hiding them along the rocky shore. A mortal man who steals a *merrow*'s cloak can keep the water fairy from returning to the sea. In many tales, this is the way mortal men trap *merrows* into becoming their wives.

Eventually these fairy wives find their cloaks, leave their mortal families, and return to their fairy world in the ocean. *Merrow* fairy wives are thought to be good housekeepers and good cooks but cold and unaffectionate to their husbands and children.

Some tales of fairy wives proclaim them to be the mates of famous rulers. In the story of the romance of Huon of Bordeaux, the fairy king Oberon tells of his mortal and fairy lineage. In a conversation with the mortal Huon, Oberon claims he is only half fairy—his mother being a fairy wife of the Roman emperor Julius Caesar.

Oberon, the fairy king, wakens his love, Titania. He is the offspring of a human father and a fairy mother. Many stories tell of beautiful fairies who married mortals.

Many historical figures were believed to be married to fairy wives. During the time of the Norman Conquest of Britain (in the tenth century), Wild Edric presented his wife, the beautiful Lady Godda, at court. Edric introduced his wife, claiming she was a fairy. Likewise, the fourteenth-century French knight Betrand du Guesclin's wife Tiphaine Raguenel of Dinant was believed to be a fairy. Rich, beautiful, and intelligent, she was called la Fee, meaning "the fairy." Legend declares that du Guesclin came upon a house in the forest. Looking in the window he saw several beautiful women dancing. He was overcome with love for the most beautiful one and he broke into the house, stealing her away. She agreed to marry him if he never asked her about her fairy sisters. Du Guesclin's fairy bride was also known to have encouraged her husband to fight for France against the English. Despite the intriguing lineage, it is possible these historical fairy wives were simply exceptional women known for their beauty and talents and had knowledge of and possessed the magical skills of the fairy faith such as herbology.

Tales of other fairy and mortal unions that do not end so positively serve as warnings against involvement with fairy women. Fairies called lamias represent the most dangerous element of the fairy realm. Lamias can appear as huge, threatening snakes but are most deadly when they become beautiful women. In one tale, a young man named Lycius of Corinth falls in love with a lamia in the disguise of a lovely woman. When Lycius is about to marry her, his mentor, a wise man, recognizes the bride to be an evil fairy. In an account of the story in the book *Fairies and Elves*, Lycius's mentor proclaims: "I will not see you made a serpent's prey. You will die in this creature's coils."[55] Hearing this, the lamia turns into a great gold and green snake who slithers away. Shortly thereafter Lycius dies of a broken heart.

A banshee flies over the Irish countryside. Many believe that the wailing of a banshee warns of imminent death.

Fairies and the Dead

Tradition, superstition, and legend are steeped with tales of the mingling of fairy and mortal lives. Many of these reported encounters are believed to have happened after the mortals die.

The purpose of Irish banshees is to warn of impending death with a long eerie wail. According to tradition, banshees follow members of well-known Irish clans wherever they live to herald a death in the family. The Irish clans of the O'Neills, the O'Briens, the O'Connors, the O'Gradys, and the Kavanaughs all are believed to have banshees following them. Banshee cries have been reported all over the world, particularly in countries such as Canada, the United States, and Australia, where many Irish immigrants settled.

Some fairy legends contend that fairies are the captors or guardians of the dead, taking them to their final destination in the afterlife. Often in the British Isles when people die, they are said to be "among the fairies." A few fairies are thought to steal the souls of dying mortals. The Irish *dullahan* is one of these. Like the banshee, the *dullahan* wails in the night. Unlike the banshee's, the *dullahan*'s wail does not warn but summons. There is no defense against the *dullahan* once the dying person hears his cry, but gold and gold artifacts are believed to keep a *dullahan* away.

Modern stories of fairy encounters seem to reflect more ancient views of fairy faith. Inspiration, natural phenomena, and respect for the earth's environment all propel the search for fairies today.

Chapter 5

The Search for Fairies

D espite the many hazards associated with fairies, people continue to seek them out in hopes of gaining some inspiration and understanding of this world and other worlds. Although questions about fairy faith, the origin of its magic, and the fairies themselves are unanswered, clues can be found throughout the British Isles. Searching for the existence of fairies and the origins of fairy beliefs leads researchers beyond hard evidence and human reports of fairy encounters into studies of history, archaeology, literature, man's relationship with the environment, and the ever-changing views on good and evil.

Clues from the Countryside

Strange and unexplained stone structures dot the countryside of the British Isles. Circles of huge, standing stones suggest primitive temples designed for ancient rituals. There are also many stone pilings built into the hills. They are known as raths, or stone forts, and many believe them to be ancient burial grounds. Who built these stone monuments remains a mystery. But local superstitions claim the stone works are the domain of the fairies and therefore should be left undisturbed.

According to many local traditions in the British Isles, fairies live in stone forts at the crests of rocky hillsides.

Most fairy sightings have occurred around these raths. In his book *Goblin Tales of Lancashire*, James Bowker reported an 1883 fairy capture in the rural hills. Allegedly, two men trying to ferret out rabbits from underground burrows near stone pilings accidentally caught a fairy named Skillywidden in their sack. Other accounts tell of people being cautious around the raths to avoid the fairies. In 1895, A.J. Evans wrote about an old man named Will Hughes and his wife Betsey in *Folklore Journal.* Will told Evans he frequently saw fairies disappearing into a hole in a hill above Rollright Circle. Betsey claimed to have put a rock over the hole when she was a child and wanted to play there "for fear the fairies would come out and frighten [her]."[56]

Stonehenge is one of several ancient monuments in the British Isles whose purpose remains unexplained. Some believe that fairies built these structures.

Those brave enough or foolish enough to interfere with a fairy rath sometimes found hidden treasures. In 1868 in Ireland, a County Limerick farmer named Quin decided to plant potatoes inside a stone fort on his land. While working, he unearthed a solid gold goblet encrusted with jewels. The find turned out to be the Ardagh Chalice, a ninth-century piece of church art. Little is known of the chalice's history but apparently it was hidden within the fort to protect it from thieves. The superstitions concerning stone raths and forts and the fairies helped keep the priceless treasure safe for more than one thousand years. The chalice is currently on exhibit at the National Museum of Ireland.

Whether or not stone monuments are fairy habitats, they can be found throughout Great Britain's countryside. And while those scattered monuments may hide small communities of fairies, many people continue to wonder about the existence of legendary fairy kingdoms like the enchanted Isle of Avalon.

The Search for Avalon

The fairy isle of Avalon's literary roots reach far beyond Britain's Arthurian legends. Avalon is named as the place where many heroes of European mythology have come to live out eternity. Described as both a paradise on Earth and a hero's heaven, the name *Avalon* actually means "Isle of Apples." According to artist and writer Brian Froud, fairy islands like Avalon have "no frosts or droughts for it is always Spring. There is no ageing or disease or work for all things grow in abundance without need of ploughing or sowing and there is always fruit on the trees."[57]

Some believe the idea of Avalon was inspired by the Fortunate Isles of Greek mythology. According to legend, these magical islands lie in the Western Sea and have orchards full of golden apples and springs flowing with nectar—the drink of the Greek gods and goddesses. Those who drink the nectar are believed to be blessed with everlasting youth and immortality. Geoffrey of Monmouth, an early author of Arthurian tales, similarly described Avalon in *Vita Merlini* as "an isle of eternal summer warmth filled with self-propagating crops, and vines that sowed themselves. There, all dwelled in peace, without illness, and lived for longer than a hundred years."[58] Geoffrey gives Avalon's geographic location as beyond the Straits of Gibraltar, suggesting it might be part of what is known today as the Canary Islands. The lure of Avalon and other magical islands, with their promises of never-ending youth and riches, was so great during the Renaissance that many explorers went looking for them in the New World.

Beliefs popular in the British Isles suggest Avalon exists much closer to home. There are numerous candidates for the mystical fairyland in and around Britain, including the Isle of Man, Bardsey Island, and Iona Island. In an ancient Irish legend, the Isle of Man is called Ablach, which means "rich in apples." Certainly, the Isle of Man is a good place for growing fruit of all kinds because gulf-stream winds keep the temperature moderate and pleasant year-round. Many stories claim Bardsey Island located off the coast of Wales is the resting place of both Merlin and King Arthur. Bardsey has held a significant place in pagan and Christian faiths and is also known as a burial place for royalty and holy men. Iona Island off of Scotland's coast has been called the Isle of Dreams, and Scottish legends claim it as Avalon.

Great Britain's most popular choice for the enchanted fairy kingdom, Glastonbury, is no longer an island. Glastonbury was once surrounded by marsh water before the land was drained. Many believe apple trees once thrived there. Glastonbury's claim as being the sight for Avalon was helped along by the monks of the Glastonbury Abbey. Beginning with the reign of Henry II in the tenth century, the monks worked for two centuries promoting artifacts and documentation declaring Glastonbury to be

The ruins of Glastonbury Abbey stand in Somerset, England. The medieval monks of the abbey claimed that Glastonbury was once the fairy island of Avalon.

the real Avalon. Historian Geoffrey Ashe wrote about the Glastonbury monks in an Internet article titled "Magical Glastonbury." By following the directions of a Welsh bard, the monks claimed to have found a stone slab with an inscription reading, "Here lies buried the renowned King Arthur in the Isle of Avalon."[59] Digging down deeper, the monks said they found the bones of a tall man. Over the years, historical records surfaced that declared Glastonbury to be Avalon. Centuries later, the documentation and the historical finds were proven false. The monks perpetuated the hoax in an attempt to attract pilgrims to Glastonbury to pay for the rebuilding of the area after much of it was destroyed by fire.

It is doubtful that Avalon as described in European mythology ever really existed. Despite evidence to the contrary, the idea of Avalon as a real place continues to fascinate many enthralled with Arthurian legends and the fairy faith. It is also doubtful powerful fairies of the Arthurian legend ever really existed. However, plenty of historical figures inspired these characters.

Historical Basis for the Fairies of the Arthurian Legend

Arthur's magical enemies and allies were all characters schooled within the fairy faith. Over the centuries, the power and purpose of these legendary characters altered to reflect changing times and the lives of historical figures. The character of Merlin was a supposed shape shifter and a powerful wizard. There is evidence suggesting Merlin was based on the life of a real pagan holy man and Welsh bard of the sixth century. Mryddin Wyllt, or Merlin the Wild, was a well-known Welsh prophet, poet, and hermit. Grief-stricken over losses at the battle of Arfderydd (Arthuret), Mryddin went insane, fleeing into the woods, where many believe he lived out his life among the wild beasts.

The powers of the female figures of Arthurian legends are similar to those of pagan goddesses and fairy faith priestesses. Over the centuries, powerful European queens also inspired authors of Arthurian tales. Two German queens served as models for the evil Morgan le Fay. One was fifth-century Queen Hildico, the wife of Atilla the Hun, who according to legend murdered her husband on their wedding night. The other, Brunhilda the Visigoth, lived during the mid-500s to the early 600s. Known to be a poisoner, political plotter, and seductress, Brunhilda married King Sigebert, who ruled eastern Germany. Brunhilda's sister married Sigebert's brother Chilperic, who ruled western Germany. War broke out between the brothers and in A.D. 575, Sigebert was assassinated and Brunhilda taken captive. Eventually Brunhilda was freed by her nephew (her captor's son) whom she married. Once again Brunhilda became a powerful queen who was responsible for the murder of at least ten kings and princes. In A.D. 613 Brunhilda was put to death by a group of German noblemen who were tired of her intrigues.

Centuries later, powerful female monarchs both influenced and financed versions of the Arthurian legend. During the mid-1100s, Eleanor of Aquitaine, while married to Henry II, encouraged music, art, and especially literature about chivalrous knights in England's royal court. Eleanor sponsored the writing of several Arthurian tales. As a result of this patronage, the female characters of the story became more prominent. Beautiful and cunning, Eleanor became a model for both King Arthur's queen, Guinevere, and Morgan le Fay, who was not yet portrayed as an evil character. Although Eleanor of Aquitaine was known to partake of political intrigue including murder (many believe she killed her husband's mistress), she inspired positive and powerful female Arthurian characters.

As the Arthurian legend evolved, its importance to British politics increased. Arthur was destined to be king because of his goodness and his upbringing in the fairy faith. For centuries, the Arthurian legend itself was considered the basis for British royalty. From William the Conqueror to Queen Victoria, British monarchs attempted to trace their roots back to King Arthur's Camelot. Perhaps the best example of an Arthurian leader was not a good king but a politically astute

Eleanor of Aquitaine, queen of England in the 1100s, was a patron of the arts. She became the model for the female characters of twelfth-century versions of Arthurian stories.

queen. Britain's Elizabeth I came to power in 1558. Like the legendary Arthur, she built up a strong military, which made England a major political force in Europe. She united her country and encouraged colonization in the New World. Queen Elizabeth presided over a relatively peaceful time in which the arts—especially literature—flourished. Another version of the Arthurian legend, *The Faerie Queene*, was written by Edmund Spenser and dedicated to Elizabeth I. In this epic poem, Spenser confirms Elizabeth's connection to the legendary Arthur and the ancient Celtic faith.

> Thy name, oh sovereign Queen, thy realm and race
> From this renowned Prince (Arthur) derived are.[60]

History, and literature inspired by history, influenced how people thought about fairies. In the mid–nineteenth century, scientific investigation began to gain popularity. At the same time, folklorists increased their studies of the spiritual world and its mystical spirits, including the fairies.

The Response to Darwin

Perhaps the book that has had the most influence on the study of fairies and the fairy faith is not a literary work but a scientific work. Often referred to as the "book that shook the world," Charles Darwin's *On the Origin of Species* sold out on its first day of publication in 1859, subsequently going through six more editions.

Darwin's theory outlined in *On the Origin of Species* maintained that the fittest of any species are more likely to survive and reproduce, creating a continuous process of evolution. It also introduced the concept that all related organisms are descended from common ancestors. For example, man is related to other primates like apes and monkeys.

The Victorian response to Darwin's theory was to study those beings and phenomena that could not be explained by scientific theory. In some cases, people who already believed in fairies presented their beliefs in terms similar to Darwin's. In his book *The Coming of the Fairies*, Sir Arthur Conan Doyle quoted a Spiritualist named Lancaster who described the fairies as "spiritual monkeys."

> They have the active brains of monkeys, and their general instinct is to avoid mankind, but they are capable individually of becoming extremely attached to humans—or a human—but at any time they may bite you, like a monkey, and repent immediately afterwards. They have thousands of years of collective experience, call it 'inherited memory' if you like, but no reasoning faculties. They are just Peter Pans—children who never grew up.[61]

In the late 1800s and early 1900s, folklorists went out to rural Ireland, Scotland, and Wales to interview people about their fairy faith and fairy encounters. What those researchers came back with explained as much about man's reaction to natural phenomena as it did about fairy faith.

Folklorist Reidar Christiansen believed fairies served a purpose by explaining life's difficult questions. In her book *The Vanishing People*, folklorist Katherine Briggs wrote that Christiansen thought the fairy beliefs "answered the questions of the untimely death of young people, of mysterious epidemics among cattle, of climatic disasters, of both wasting diseases and strokes, of infantile paralysis."[62]

Some researchers accepted unquestioningly the existence of fairies. W.Y. Evans Wentz, an American of Celtic descent and author of *The Fairy Faith in Celtic Countries*,

Charles Darwin introduced the theory of evolution in his On the Origin of Species. *Spiritualists used Darwin's work as a model for their own theories on fairies.*

thought the fairies were nature spirits whose existence and powers were understood by ancient pagan priests. "These experiences of mine [interviews with believers] lead me to believe that the natural aspects of Celtic countries impress man and awaken in him some unfamiliar part of himself," wrote Evans Wentz. "Which gives him [mankind] an unusual power to know and to feel invisible, or psychical [psychic] influences [like the fairies]."[63] The fact that Evans Wentz and other researchers accepted fairies as real helped them when interviewing rural people; those interviewed felt comfortable opening up to other believers. What these turn-of-the-century researchers compiled was a comprehensive study of people's many beliefs about fairies.

The fairies represented an important connection to Great Britain's past. The studies and renewed interest in the fairies were a result of the increased pride in all things British, including the mythology and folklore of the British Isles.

The Cottingley Fairies

Myths, folklore, and superstitions give little proof of fairy and human encounters. Two young English girls attempted to change that in the early 1900s. In the summer of 1917, sixteen-year-old Elsie Wright and her ten-year-old cousin, Frances Griffiths, claimed to have taken pictures of fairies in the glen in Cottingley, a place near Bradford in Yorkshire. The two had played in the glen for years. When Elsie told her parents about seeing fairies there, her father teased her. She decided to prove him wrong by photographing the sprites.

When developed, Elsie's pictures did have "fairies" in them. The fairies looked only inches high, with childlike faces and short dresses—not much like the descriptions rural people had given researchers ten years earlier. However, Elsie's mother, a Spiritualist, believed her daughter had photographed the fairies in the glen. A few years later in 1920, the mother took Elsie's photographs to Edward Gardner, a sometime associate of British author Sir Arthur Conan Doyle. Gardner interviewed Elsie and was impressed by her directness. But he still wanted more evidence, so he arranged for the girls to take more pictures in "controlled conditions"—using marked photographic plates that could not be substituted. In August of 1920, the girls took more photographs. Elsie and Frances were always left alone during these photo sessions to ensure adult onlookers would not disturb the fairies. All the pictures taken by the girls had fairies in them and appeared unaltered.

Gardner then showed the photographs to Doyle, who agreed that they captured real fairies on film. Doyle, a member of a spiritualist society, was an "expert" on psychic phenomena as well as a famous writer. As the creator of the

A photo shows Frances Griffiths among fairies in Cottingley, England. Griffiths and her cousin, Elsie Wright, took many photos as proof that they had seen fairies.

brilliant and rational master sleuth Sherlock Holmes, Doyle gave the children's claim more credulity and publicity. Both Gardner and Doyle wrote about the pictures, and Doyle's book *The Coming of the Fairies* was published in 1923. The 1997 film *Fairy Tale: A True Story* is based on the Cottingley fairy incident.

It was not until the 1980s, when an elderly Elsie and Frances admitted to pinning up cutouts of fairies to photograph, that the incident was declared a hoax. Still, the general public's view of fairies would never be the same. The once powerful and magical beings of Celtic mythology were now tiny sprites relegated to quaint childhood tales.

Fairies and Light

Oftentimes described as luminous beings seemingly of another world, fairies have long been associated with unearthly spirits and unexplained sources of light. According to many reports of fairy sightings, light seems to both attract and encompass the mystical fairies. Many see fairies as forms of light as well as being surrounded by light. In *A Complete Guide to Faeries and Magical Beings*, Cassandra Eason reports on several sightings of luminous fairies. Five-year-old Andrew told his mother about two small fairies he had seen in his school's corridor. Andrew claimed one fairy gave off green light, the other blue light. "The fairy beings were in the center of the light that became paler the further away the light was from them. They went by very quickly, one in front of the other as if they were playing tag."[64] A modern-day Druid named Melvyn described fairies he claimed to see at a pagan festival as being part of the light. "It was as if someone had lit a giant sparkler and all the light beams were flying around."[65]

Fairies are also believed to be drawn to strange sources of light called earth lights. Sometimes referred to as Will O' the wisps or Longdendale lights, the ancient phenomenon of earth lights is associated with both European fairy folk and Native American little people. Earth lights glow and hover not far from the ground. At times, they appear as circles of light; at other times, as luminous brush strokes across the sky. Some scientists believe earth lights result from spontaneous combustion of decaying matter over grassy marshlands. Other scientists think earth lights could emanate from geological faults in the earth. Modern-day fairy faith practitioners claim earth lights are attracted to pagan festivals and the ancient stone monuments of the British Isles.

Some believe both the lights and the fairies are energy fields surrounding undisturbed countrysides. This theory corresponds with ancient Celtic beliefs—that fairies are elements of nature and can be called upon through various pagan rituals. The connection between phenomena in the natural world, the fairies, and Great Britain's past is evident in the research gathered from rural areas within the last century.

A few researchers have suggested fairies descended from real races of people who once lived within certain regions of the British Isles. It is believed as groups intermarried, traces of these fairy races were lost through assimilation with other groups and the modern world.

The Flower Fairy Artist

Besides inspiring magical tales, fairies also inspire luminous art. One artist moved by the fairies took cues from her lovely flower garden and neighboring schoolchildren. Cicely Mary Barker was born in London in 1895. As a child, she was sickly but found happiness in drawing and painting the world around her. The imaginary world of the fairies inspired her to do her best-known work—a collection of flower fairy books first published in 1923.

She found models for her flower fairies from the children who attended her sister's kindergarten. Her watercolor illustrations depict accurate details of many flowers alongside the fairies that watch over them.

Barker painted flower fairies for fifty years. Her work has convinced many children and adults to look carefully for the fairies in their own flower gardens.

The Case for Human Fairy Races

Some early-twentieth-century researchers thought a group of dwarfish people once lived in the caves and stone forts of ancient Ireland, Scotland, and Wales. Supposedly, these ancient little people hunted with flint arrows and were believed to have control over the weather and possess other magical powers.

Researcher J.F. Campbell thought British house elves—better known as "brownies"—possibly descended from a race of little people who lived in woods and mounds but hung around farms. Later, they were conquered by the ancient Celts. This group, Campbell asserts, ended up serving their captors by providing them with gifts of food. One of the main reasons Campbell came to this conclusion was that the brownie stories were so widely spread and matter of fact. As quoted in Katherine Briggs's book *The Vanishing People*, Campbell said, "I am persuaded of the former existence of a race of men in these islands who were smaller in stature than the Celts; who used stone arrows, lived in conical mounds like the Lapps [of northern Norway and Sweden], knew some mechanical arts, pilfered goods and stole children."[66]

A few modern researchers have wondered if some Native American little people might also have descended from a real race of people. Along the Venezuela-Colombia border, Yupa tribal members tell tales of a race of pygmies called the Pipintu. The Pipintu live among the Yupa but within their own family groups. According to Yupa folklore, the Pipintu once lived underground, becoming fully human only after intermarrying with the Yupa.

Most modern-day researchers do not believe fairies were ever actual human beings. However, human qualities, human history, and human beliefs in deities have all combined to create the different perspectives on what fairies are. As supernatural beings, fairies have gained respect in a world whose natural resources are dwindling.

Making Room for the Fairies

Respect for the fairies and those who believe in them is still common in places like rural Ireland—especially among the elderly. In Ireland in 1959, community protests changed the route of a road at Toorglas in County Mayo. The proposed road would have cut through what many believed was a fairy palace. The road builders themselves went on strike rather than destroy the fairy habitat. When the head of the road commission met with local farmers, he was told that although the farmers did not believe in the fairies, they would also oppose the road's route out of respect for the believers and local superstitions. The road's course was changed and the fairy fort saved.

Today, people are working to save fairy habitats by saving the remaining rural countryside—for it seems positive encounters with fairies are more likely to occur in nature. A Berkshire, England, woman named Lilian explained her friendly meetings with fairies to writer Cassandra Eason. Lilian claimed to have seen fairies during her childhood vacation to the countryside in the 1940s. "I got very close to nature and began to be aware of the presences in the countryside around me," said Lilian. "I started to use my will power to bring out the essences of these presences. I was aware even then that other people did not have time to see [the fairies]."[67]

Environmental conservation is a major concern of the growing number of modern pagan groups like the Green Circle, the Order of Bards, Ovates, Druids, and the Ring of Troth. These New Age groups also work to preserve and renew ancient pagan religions. Most claim to believe in ancient gods and goddesses including powerful nature spirits like the fairies. In his book *Glamoury*, Steve Blamires writes about the renewed interest in ancient pagan beliefs and nature spirits and how they relate to life today:

A painting shows a fairy singing in a forest. Many people believe that protecting such areas from development will ensure the future of fairies.

From this acceptance of the ebb and flow of life, they began to understand how these cycles are deeply related to individual growth. As time passed, they couched their wisdom in a huge body of legends, many of which have been passed down to us through the generations. These legends, which cradle the wisdom of the great Celtic magical tradition, have survived the centuries because humans have always instinctively recognized their essential truth and validity.[68]

Some modern-day practitioners of the fairy faith build new fairy habitats by nurturing gardens. As Yorskire wise-woman Claire O'Rush espouses:

> There are many kinds of fairies at work in the world, and to attract them into our garden we have to learn to pour love into its heart, so that we cherish every living thing within its precincts. Even those insects and animals we would discourage need to be thanked for playing their part in nature's cycle before they are humanely banished. This approach will draw us closer to the fairies.[69]

As more and more rural land is cleared, fewer and fewer fairy sightings are being recorded. Still, people claim to find fairies working within their lives and on rare occasions some people find what could be solid evidence of fairy existence.

The Fairy Shoe

Throughout the British Isles, fairies are respected by being referred to as the "good people" or the "good neighbors." Superstitions claim fairies are more likely to trick nonbelievers than believers. Everyone is familiar with the superstitions—even nonbelievers know it is better not to tempt fate by interferring with a fairy rath, hill, or tree. However, sometimes even the most careful of mortals comes across what appears to be fairy artifacts. In 1834, a farm laborer found a small shoe while working in southwestern Ireland. Fearing the shoe belonged to the fairies and would bring him bad luck, the farm laborer gave it away. Throughout the next century and a half, the shoe was passed down to many different people.

Currently the shoe is in the possession of an Irishman named Charles Somerville. Interviewed for a documentary produced for The Learning Channel called *Legends of Ireland: Fairies and Leprechauns*, Somerville said he had taken the shoe to both a curator of a doll museum and a cobbler. The museum curator told Somerville the workmanship on the shoe was too intricate to be a doll shoe. According to the curator, the condition of the shoe suggested it had actually been worn. The cobbler told Somerville he doubted any human shoemaker could have made the shoe. "He [the cobbler] said the work was as good as any cobbler could do. Indeed better because the shoe was so small,"[70] said Somerville. The cobbler saw that the shoe had been mended. It appeared that at one time the shoe had laces because it had tiny eyelet holes.

Somerville did not say whether or not he believed in fairies. But he was curious about the shoe. "I suppose I should snip a bit of the leather and have it tested, but somehow I don't think the fairies would like that."[71]

Today's converts to the fairy faith do not seek out fairies but find them within their everyday lives. For many artists and poets, fairies inspire and provoke the imagination. But fairies are too elusive to ever provide proof of their existence. "Between light and darkness, legend creates dusk," wrote Pierre Dubois in *The Great Encyclopedia of Faeries*. "This dusk becomes faerieland. . . . With these

Alien Fairies

One of the earliest reported space alien sightings in the United States happened on a farm just outside of Hopskinville, Kentucky, in 1955. But to those who claimed to have seen them, these aliens did not look like they came from outer space. They looked like they emerged from a nearby fairy hill or stone fairy fort. Small, with dark, wrinkled skin and large ears and eyes, these goblinlike creatures were reportedly attacking humans. Witnesses alleged five of the alien beings approached a farmer and his family. Out of fear, the farmer took aim with his rifle and shot at one of them. The farmer claimed the bullet bounced off the creature's chest as if it had hit hard metal. When a family member went to investigate the situation, he claimed he was touched by a silvery hand just before the alien elves disappeared. The strange beings became known as the Hopskinville goblins.

confused, flashing fragments the Faeries will build a king-dom of the Dawn."[72] The search for fairies begins with legend and ends in mystery.

Out of Sight but Not Out of Mind

Some believe fairies hold great power over mortals. According to author Evans Wentz, "The fairy race had the power to destroy half the human race yet refrained from doing so out of ethical considerations."[73] It would seem the opposite is true as the modern world encroaches upon fairy habitat. Yet the dwindling countryside makes people yearn for nature's beauty and the magic associated with the fairies.

Others contend fairies are at best nuisances, not really mysterious nor particularly powerful. In 1909, Sophia Morrison, a well-known folklorist on the Island of Man, wrote about how she believed that fairies were simply unexplained natural phenomena. Morrison hoped that someday researchers would understand fairies like they came to understand the technology behind X rays and wireless telegraphs. But it is apparent that the mystery of the fairies is far from being solved.

Whether imagination creates the fairies, or fairies spark the imagination, people are fascinated with them. Their powers may have decreased from ancient myths to modern fairy tales, but for many the possibility of their existence remains in the ring of windswept leaves or the blossoming of a tiny flower. Real or imagined, fairies have become part of human life through folklore, literature, and belief. As such, they continue to inspire and confound human beings.

Notes

Introduction: The Little People of the Countryside

1. Quoted in Katherine Briggs, *The Vanishing People: Fairy Lore and Legends.* New York: Pantheon, 1978, p. 51.

Chapter One: What Are Fairies?

2. Quoted in W.Y. Evans Wentz, *The Fairy Faith in Celtic Countries.* New York: Oxford University Press, 1911, p. 29.
3. Quoted in Evans Wentz, *The Fairy Faith in Celtic Countries*, p. 30.
4. Briggs, *The Vanishing People*, p. 51.
5. Quoted in Brian Froud and Alan Lee, *Faeries.* New York: Harry N. Abrams, 1978, p. 68.
6. Briggs, *The Vanishing People*, p. 5.
7. Froud and Lee, *Faeries*, p. 2.
8. Quoted in Brian Froud, *Good Faeries, Bad Faeries.* New York: Simon and Schuster, 1998, p. 17.
9. Quoted in Froud, *Good Faeries, Bad Faeries*, p. 17.
10. Quoted in Evans Wentz, *The Fairy Faith in Celtic Countries*, p. 60.
11. Quoted in Froud and Lee, *Faeries*, p. 62.
12. Froud and Lee, *Faeries*, p. 63.
13. Quoted in William Aldis Wright, ed., *The Complete Works of William Shakespeare.* Philadelphia, PA: Doubleday, Doran, 1936, p. 813.
14. Ann Moura, *Green Witchcraft: Folk Magic, Fairy Lore and Herb Craft.* St. Paul, MN: Llewellyn, 1997, p. 86.

Chapter Two: The Origins of Fairy Folk

15. Quoted in Carole G. Silver, *Strange and Secret Peoples: Fairies and Victorian Consciousness.* New York: Oxford University Press, 1999, p. 188.
16. Quoted in Briggs, *The Vanishing People*, p. 35.
17. Quoted in Evans Wentz, *The Fairy Faith in Celtic Countries*, p. 32.
18. Quoted in Briggs, *The Vanishing People*, p. 32.
19. Froud, *Good Faeries, Bad Faeries*, p. 3.
20. Briggs, *The Vanishing People*, p. 17.
21. Pierre Dubois, *The Great Encyclopedia of Faeries.* New York: Simon and Schuster, 2000, p. 138.
22. Dubois, *The Great Encyclopedia of Faeries*, p. 12.
23. Dubois, *The Great Encyclopedia of Faeries*, p. 13.
24. Dubois, *The Great Encyclopedia of Faeries*, p. 13.
25. Quoted in Briggs, *The Vanishing People*, p. 31.

Chapter Three: The Evolution of the Fairy Faith

26. Quoted in Kent, *The Complete Works of William Shakespeare*, p. 391.
27. Quoted in Steve Blamires, *Glamoury:*

Magic of the Celtic Green World. St. Paul, MN: Llewellyn, 1995, p. 19.

28. Quoted in Blamires, *Glamoury*, p. 19.

29. John Matthews, *The Druid Source Book.* London: Blandford, 1996, p. 239.

30. David Day, *The Search for King Arthur.* New York: Facts On File, 1998, p. 65.

31. Claire O'Rush, *The Enchanted Garden: Discovering and Enhancing the Magical Healing Properties in Your Garden.* New York: Gramercy Books, 1996, p. 23.

32. Quoted in Kent, *The Complete Works of William Shakespeare*, p. 427.

33. Quoted in Cassandra Eason, *A Complete Guide to Faeries and Magical Beings.* Boston: Weiser Books, 2002, p. 170.

34. John Bierhorst, *The Deetkatoo: Native American Stories about Little People.* New York: William Morrow, 1998, p. vi.

35. Bierhorst, *The Deetkatoo*, p. xviii.

36. Quoted in Bierhorst, *The Deetkatoo*, p. xv.

37. O'Rush, *The Enchanted Garden*, p. 8.

38. Blamires, *Glamoury*, p. xvii.

39. Blamires, *Glamoury*, p. 55.

Chapter Four: Human Encounters with Fairies

40. Quoted in Ward Rutherford, *Celtic Lore: The History of the Druids and Their Timeless Traditions.* San Francisco, CA: Thorsons, 1993, p. 127.

41. Froud, *Good Faeries, Bad Faeries*, p. 7.

42. Froud, *Good Faeries, Bad Faeries*, p. 5.

43. Quoted in O'Rush, *The Enchanted Garden*, p. 27.

44. Quoted in Eason, *A Complete Guide to Faeries and Magical Beings*, p. 51.

45. Quoted in Eason, *A Complete Guide to Faeries and Magical Beings*, p. 50.

46. Moura, *Green Witchcraft*, p. 87.

47. Quoted in Evans Wentz, *The Fairy Faith in Celtic Countries*, p. 32.

48. Quoted in Briggs, *The Vanishing People*, p. 40.

49. Quoted in Eason, *A Complete Guide to Faeries and Magical Beings*, p. 66.

50. Froud, *Good Faeries, Bad Faeries*, p. 5.

51. Bob Curran, *A Field Guide to Irish Fairies.* San Francisco, CA: Chronicle Books, 1998, p. 32.

52. Quoted in Curran, *A Field Guide to Irish Fairies*, p. 33.

53. Quoted in Briggs, *The Vanishing People*, p. 103.

54. Quoted in Curran, *A Field Guide to Irish Fairies*, p. 44.

55. Quoted in *The Enchanted World: Fairies and Elves*, Alexandria, VA: Time-Life Books, 1984, p. 117.

Chapter Five: The Search for Fairies

56. Quoted in Briggs, *The Vanishing People*, p. 88.

57. Froud and Lee, *Faeries*, p. 29.

58. Quoted in Day, *The Search for King Arthur*, p. 151.

59. Quoted in Geoffrey Ashe, "Magical Glastonbury," 1999. www.brittania.com.

60. Quoted in Day, *The Search for King Arthur*, p. 161.

61. Quoted in Sir Arthur Conan Doyle, *The Coming of the Fairies.* London: Pavillion Books, 1997, p. 88.

62. Briggs, *The Vanishing People*, p. 28.

63. Quoted in Eason, *A Complete Guide to Faeries and Magical Beings*, p. 43.

64. Quoted in Eason, *A Complete Guide to Faeries and Magical Beings*, p. 52.
65. Quoted in Eason, *A Complete Guide to Faeries and Magical Beings*, p. 44.
66. Quoted in Briggs, *The Vanishing People*, p. 105.
67. Quoted in Eason, *A Complete Guide to Faeries and Magical Beings*, p. xiv.
68. Blamires, *Glamoury*, p. 1.
69. O'Rush, *The Enchanted Garden*, p. 22.
70. Quoted in The Learning Channel, *Legends of Ireland: Fairies and Leprechauns*, Emdee Productions, 1998.
71. Quoted in The Learning Channel, *Legends of Ireland: Fairies and Leprechauns*.
72. Dubois, *The Great Encyclopedia of Faeries*, p. 12.
73. Quoted in Froud, *Good Faeries, Bad Faeries*, p. 8.

For Further Reading

Michael Hague, *The Book of Fairies*. New York: HarperCollins Children's Books, 2000. Beautifully illustrated collection of stories, songs, and poetry about the fairies.

Eloise McGraw, *The Moorchild*. New York: Margaret K. McElderry Books, 1996. Newberry honoree book about a young girl who is half human, half fairy and has difficulty fitting in in the mortal world.

Francis Melville, *The Book of Faeries: A Guide to the World of Elves, Pixies, Goblins, and Other Magical Spirits*. Hauppauge, NY: Barrons Educational Series, 2002. This book presents history and folklore surrounding fairies and discusses the origins of fairies in different cultures.

Gossamer Penwyche, *The World of Fairies*. London: Sterling, 2003. This book describes different types of fairies and includes their cultural significance.

Elizabeth Ratisseau, *Fairies*. London: Sterling, 2001. This book presents fairy paintings and includes select quotations with each artwork.

Suza Scalora, *The Fairies: Photographic Evidence of the Existence of Another World*. New York: Joanna Colter Books, 1999. A book with elegant and elaborate photographs of what the author imagines fairies to be like in today's world. Each photograph is accompanied by a log of the author's travels to locate the fairies.

Paul Robert Walker, *Little Folk: Stories from Around the World*. San Diego, CA: Harcourt Brace, 1997. A retelling of many stories about fairies from many different cultures. Each tale includes background and history of the culture it came from.

Works Consulted

Books

John Bierhorst, *The Deetkatoo: Native American Stories about Little People.* New York: William Morrow, 1998. Excellent book explaining the origins of Native American little people. It includes several folktales.

Steve Blamires, *Glamoury: Magic of the Celtic Green World.* St. Paul, MN: Llewellyn Publications, 1995. Blamires explains ancient Celtic practices and modern-day versions of the fairy faith in a simple and readable fashion.

Katherine Briggs, *An Encyclopedia of Fairies: Hobgoblins, Brownies, Bogies and Other Supernatural Creatures.* New York: Pantheon Books, 1976. This is a good reference book on the subject of fairies.

———, *The Vanishing People: Fairy Lore and Legends.* New York: Pantheon, 1978. An excellent analysis of fairy faith, origins, and folklore.

Bob Curran, *A Field Guide to Irish Fairies.* San Francisco, CA: Chronicle Books, 1998. Fun and whimsically illustrated, this book describes a variety of fairies, their natures, and their effects on mortals.

David Day, *The Search for King Arthur.* New York: Facts On File, 1998. A fascinating book outlining the origins and influences surrounding the Arthurian legend.

Sir Arthur Conan Doyle, *The Coming of the Fairies.* London: Pavillion Books, 1997. A reprint of Doyle's original work concerning the Cottingley fairies. Portions of other interviews on fairy beliefs and encounters are also included.

Pierre Dubois, *The Great Encyclopedia of Faeries.* New York: Simon and Schuster, 2000. Beautifully illustrated and poetically written, this book describes many kinds of fairies from all over the world.

Cassandra Eason, *A Complete Guide to Faeries and Magical Beings.* Boston, MA: Weiser Books, 2002. This book covers all matter of beliefs in fairies.

W.Y. Evans Wentz, *The Fairy Faith in Celtic Countries.* New York: Oxford University Press, 1911. Although the writing is antiquated, this is the most comprehensive study of research on the fairy faith in the early 1900s.

Brian Froud, *Good Faeries, Bad Faeries.* New York: Simon and Schuster, 1998. Well illustrated, this book offers a creative view of both good and evil fairies.

Brian Froud and Alan Lee, *Faeries*. New York: Harry N. Abrams, 1978. An imaginative yet thorough account of fairy origins and fairy lore.

Carol K. Mack and Dinah Mack, *A Field Guide to Demons, Fairies, Fallen Angels, and Other Subversive Spirits*. New York: Arcade, 1998. Good resource book on the subject of fairies.

John Matthews, *The Druid Source Book*. London: Blandford, 1996. Essays on ancient Celts and their religious practices.

Ann Moura, *Green Witchcraft: Folk Magic, Fairy Lore and Herb Craft*. St. Paul, MN: Llewellyn, 1997. Written from the perspective of a modern-day fairy faith practitioner, this book discusses everyday encounters between humans and fairies.

Claire O'Rush, *The Enchanted Garden: Discovering and Enhancing the Magical Healing Properties in Your Garden*. New York: Gramercy Books, 1996. This is a beautifully illustrated book describing the fairy faith as it has evolved over the past two centuries.

Carol Rose, *Spirits, Fairies, Gnomes, and Goblins: An Encyclopedia of the Little People*. Santa Barbara, CA: ABC-CLIO, 1996. An excellent and comprehensive resource book on fairies from all over the world.

Ward Rutherford, *Celtic Lore: The History of the Druids and Their Timeless Traditions*. San Francisco, CA: Thorsons, 1993. Comprehensive history of Great Britain and the fairy faith.

Carole G. Silver, *Strange and Secret Peoples: Fairies and Victorian Consciousness*. New York: Oxford University Press, 1999. Discusses literature, politics, and the fairy faith during the Victorian era.

Time-Life Books, eds., *The Enchanted World: Fairies and Elves*. Alexandria, VA: Time-Life Books, 1984. This volume describes different fairies and includes several folktales.

Frederick Warne, *A World of Flower Fairies*. London: Penguin Books, 1992. A book of poems and watercolor illustrations by Cicely Mary Barker that capture the whimsical and beautiful flower fairies.

William Aldis Wright, ed., *The Complete Works of William Shakespeare*. Philadelphia, PA: Doubleday, Doran, 1936. This Shakespeare collection includes synopses of the plays and origins of their plots.

Internet Sources

Geoffrey Ashe, "Magical Glastonbury," 1999. www.britannia.com. An Internet article that discusses Glastonbury's pagan, Christian, and modern history.

Rebecca Lawrence, "Druidry and the Druids," Church of Tylwyth Teg, 2001. www.tylwthteg.com. Internet article written about ancient Druids by a modern-day Druid.

Video

The Learning Channel, *Legends of Ireland: Fairies and Leprechauns*, Emdee Productions, 1998. Explanations for the fairy shoe and the Ardagh Chalice are presented within this documentary. It also includes commentary from many prominent historians and folklorists.

Index

Picture Credits

Cover photo: © Christie's Images/CORBIS

© Paul Almasy/CORBIS, 68

© Art Resource, NY, 34

© Bettmann/CORBIS, 47, 53, 87

© Blue Lantern Studio/CORBIS, 12, 27

© Cynthia Hart Designer/CORBIS, 23

© Historical Picture Archive/CORBIS, 44

Hulton/Archive by Getty Images, 73, 78, 81, 83

© Image Club, 9, 14, 26, 62

© Erich Lessing/Art Resource, NY, 37, 39

Library of Congress, 51, 85

Mary Evans Picture Library, 16, 49, 64, 67, 70, 75

© Gregory McCarthy/CORBIS, 20

North Wind Picture Archives, 30

Prints Old and Rare, 56

© Royalty-Free/CORBIS, 41

© Snark/Art Resource, NY, 92

© Stapleton Collection/CORBIS, 35

About the Author

Nancy Hoffman has written several books including *Heart Transplants* (part of Lucent's Great Medical Discovery series), *West Virginia, South Carolina*, and *Eleanor Roosevelt and the Arthurdale Experiment*. She lives in Nashville, Tennessee, with her husband Tony and daughters Eva and Chloe.